WHAT IS LOVE?

50 questions about how to find, keep, and rediscover it

ANDREW G. MARSHALL

MARSHALL METHOD
PUBLISHING

The letters in this book are from people who have written to me via my website and the case histories are based on persons with whom I have worked in my therapy practice. Their details have been changed to protect confidentiality.

Marshall Publishing Method
London • Florida
www.marshallmethodpublishing.com

ISBN: 978-0-9929718-0-9

Cover and interior design: Gary A. Rosenberg • www.thebookcouple.com

Printed and bound by CPI Group (UK) Ltd, Croydon, CR0 4YY

CONTENTS

INTRODUCTION

It all seems so simple in the movies. Boy meets girl and, although they might not immediately recognise that they were 'made for each other', after a few misunderstandings and a couple of obstacles, they will fall in love and get married. The only question is whether they are *truly* in love. If they've passed this test—which is seldom in doubt because they're the hero and heroine—they will always triumph. There are sometimes ex-lovers or rivals but they are normally painted as 'bad' people and so either disappear before the happy ending or miraculously discover someone else in the final frames of the story. No wonder we believe love will overcome, especially if—another movie myth—we follow our heart and really believe in its power. Therefore we never really consider the truth about love but instead sink into the comforting embrace of the myths and stories we tell ourselves (over and over again).

If you've bought or are browsing through this book, my guess is that real life has punctured all your cosy expectations and happily ever after turned out to be complicated, messy and painful. Perhaps your beloved has dumped you and you're questioning whether he or she ever really loved you. Maybe it's you that *thought* you loved your partner but now you're not quite so sure. Perhaps your husband or wife has been unfaithful but claims that he or she still loves you and you're wondering 'How does that work?' Maybe you are torn and have 'feelings' for both your partner and a colleague at work, someone you've met on the Internet or your childhood sweetheart. Whatever the circumstances, you have lots of pressing questions about love: what is it, what went wrong and can I ever get it back?

While you have no shortage of questions, you're short on answers. Your partner can't explain and if he or she does come up with something to explain the change of heart it simply doesn't makes sense. If you ask a counsellor, you'll probably get the questions turned back with 'What do you think?' Meanwhile philosophers quote the ancient Greeks and poets are more interested in chronicling the pains and pleasures of love than offering solutions. No wonder you're feeling lost, frustrated and angry. Should love really be this difficult? Whatever happened to 'being swept off your feet'? What about 'my happily ever after'?

Fortunately, I've spent almost 30 years as a marital therapist trying to understand the truth about love and make it work in the real world. I've also written numerous books on the subject—including the international best seller: *I Love You But I'm Not In Love With You*. Countless people have written to my website posing questions very similar to yours and I've done my best to provide not only insights but hope and solutions.

I've decided to gather these letters into a book because I think these dispatches from the coalface of love will help. Firstly, it's reassuring to realise that you're not alone and that other people's lives are not like the movies either. Secondly, reading someone else's story can help you see your own more clearly. Thirdly, it will help you step into other people's shoes and, as you'll discover, that's a really useful relationship skill.

Time and again, my correspondents fear there are just two choices: putting up, shutting up and enduring, or running away and starting again. However, I believe there are countless other outcomes because people can change. I hope the range of experiences in this book and seeing opinions from different sides of the same dilemma will illustrate this central belief. Although I'm tackling the individual circumstances—based on experience of counselling similar cases and my intuition—I've also tried to make general points, teach relationship skills and open minds.

How to use this book

The letters are arranged into themes but I would recommend reading them all—not just the most pertinent ones—because every question illuminates another aspect of love. I sum up the possible lesson from each letter with a definition of love. At the back of the book, I've gathered together my thoughts and answered the central question that underlines everybody's dilemma: what is love? I finish with an exercise to help you pull together everything that has challenged, surprised or provided a fresh insight. In this way, if you're at an emotional crossroads or you and your partner are currently at odds over love, my book will help to stop you going round in circles and to signpost a way forward.

Andrew G. Marshall
www.andrewgmarshall.com

THE QUESTIONS

FINDING LOVE

1. I am a 36-year-old woman who has never had a serious relationship. The longest I've ever gone out with a man is two
weeks. Many people consider me attractive and I've been told by
acquaintances and strangers that I am beautiful. I hardly ever find
the men who are interested in me physically attractive, which is
important to me, I cannot be intimate with someone who does not
attract me.

The men I've been with—two or three casual flings—over the
past 18 years have this in common: I've always been very sexually
attracted to them, they make the initial approach, have always
been witty and amusing, but then it turns into a situation where I
get obsessed and throw myself at them. I become needy and too
compliant instead of being true to myself. Even though I have had
sexual relationships, I have never been able to have full penetra-
tive sex. I've always found it too painful.

My last fling was nearly nine years ago. It was with a work colleague who kept our sexual relationship secret which hurt me
greatly. The last time I kissed a man was four years ago at a friend's
wedding. When he asked for my phone number the next day, I
was cold and stiff to him even though I was attracted to him.
Needless to say he never rang me, and I don't blame him.

I work long hours so my social life is restricted and I feel too old for nightclubs. I tried internet dating—my friend met her partner in this way—but I never felt comfortable doing it. My father is a very handsome man. He is a good father but he has a short fuse so he could quickly turn from being good-humoured to being angry and sulky. My brother who is a year younger than I has minor learning difficulties. Growing up that was hard for the family to deal with. We've never really talked about it, least of all my brother. My younger sister is happily married.

Thank you for your time.

Andrew writes:

First off, I want to reassure you. There are lots of people in the same situation who have reached their thirties and sometimes even forties without having a single long-term relationship and only a handful of flings. I call this 'under-dating' and I think it is one of the hidden phenomena of our times.

So why does it happen? As you point out in your letter, there are family issues—normally a difficult father or an absent mother. But I've noticed quite a few women with brothers with mental or physical health issues who swallow a lot of attention and the daughter has been sidelined or felt compelled to be 'perfect' or 'get on with things' as the family can't cope with any more problems.

The result is that relationships are both very attractive—a chance to be centre stage in someone's life—but very threatening too (as when you get close to someone it is easy to be hurt or rejected). So how do you cope with being simultaneously attracted and frightened by intimacy? There are two ways of coping. In the first, you blow hot (and have a passionate kiss) and then cold (the next morning when he asks for your number) so the potential boyfriends don't know where they stand. Alternatively, you become over-committed (almost straight-away) to someone who is unavailable, blows hot or cold himself or might be up for a relationship but is simply overwhelmed because events move too quickly. (Don't worry if this sounds bleak because understanding these dances of commitment is a big step forward to stopping doing them.)

However, there is an extra twist—which I think you follow. You put so much emphasis on that initial bolt of attraction because somehow the power of this moment will bond you together forever and his sheer gorgeousness will keep you locked in love. This might happen in fairy tales but I've never met one single couple that fit this description (and I've been in this game for almost 30 years).

In reality, love moves through six stages from initial attraction to a lifetime of togetherness—each with its own challenge and needing its own skill set. Poets and pop song writers concentrate on the first one—which I call *Blending* (two people merge into one couple)—because it is the most dramatic. Let me explain what's happening. To help us overcome our fears and the irrationality of trusting our future to a complete stranger, our bodies are flooded with bonding chemicals (like oxytocin and dopamine) and we have that walking on air, can't sleep, can't eat or do anything but think about our beloved or have passionate sex together! Psychologists call this effect limerence and the important thing to realise is that it doesn't last forever; in most cases somewhere between six months (when our feelings are not returned) and three years (when a couple fall in love and mutually reinforce the feelings).

The second stage is called *Nesting*—which normally kicks in around the second or third year—where a couple show their love by moving in together. Slowly but surely, they become aware there's more to a relationship than kissing, cuddling and sex, and setting up a home becomes a new way of expressing their love. The third stage, which is around the third or fourth year, I call *Self-Affirming* because couples realise that there is an 'I' as well as a 'we' and it doesn't take two people to go to the DIY store to choose a screwdriver. Some people find this difficult because there are more arguments, but without this stage we'd lose our sense of personal identity.

By five to 14 years into a relationship, which I call *Collaborating,* couples use their new found security to launch joint projects which provide a common purpose and feed their relationship. The most common choice is having children but it could be starting a business, renovating a cottage or travelling together. Stage five is *Adapting,* which spans from approximately 15–25 years, and is about coping with the changes life throws at us rather than internal changes within the relationship—for example, elderly parents needing more care and children leaving home. The final stage, *Renewing,* is an echo of the first one, and the reason why elderly couples are the most romantic and everything to each other. While during *Blending,* the closeness is based on the promise of a life together—with *Renewing,* it is based on the reality.

Of course, attraction is an important ingredient for keeping a relationship healthy during this journey—but only one of them. You need respect, consideration, compassion, shared interests, friendship and laughter. However, most important of all, is the ability to communicate properly and sort out the inevitable differences along the way. In fact lots of happy couples hardly notice their partner when they first meet—just that he or she is interesting or quite nice. Some are friends or colleagues—and there's not even the beginning of a spark—but discover love along the way. In this way, the connection is based on the reality of each other rather than a shared fantasy.

Maybe, if you give yourself time to get to know one of these guys who finds you attractive, you'll find him interesting on the second or third look. If you can talk to him about your fears, let the trust build up and take it one step at a time, who knows what will develop... It's much better than asking yourself on first acquaintance, do I want to spend the rest of my life with this man? With the stakes this high, your anxiety will kick in and of course the answer will be NO.

What is love? *More than just a blinding attraction.*

2.

I'm 38 and I've been single for 10+ years. Dates and so on; nothing serious.

My life is totally different to what I ever imagined—in some very positive ways. Life is generally good—fun activities, wide range of friends, emotionally closer to family, etc. The negative side is I just never expected to be single.

A couple of my friends totally disappeared into relationships and haven't resurfaced. Others have returned now their kids are older. I've often felt like a catalyst for others to meet, which I mostly like. But I don't want to be a leftover for the rest of my life.

I sometimes picture being 80 in my old folks' home welcoming old friends who've lost their partners but slightly resenting, underneath, that they deserted me for so long. I worked in an old folks' home as a teen and there are waaaay more women than men at that age.

The guy I thought I'd marry died in a motorcycle accident when I lived in the US (I'm a native). We'd been on-and-off for about five years and we'd always said we'd get married when we were 30. He died about two months before his 29th birthday. Some irrational part of me acts like he intentionally died in the ambulance. As in, he stopped trying to live (as opposed to the reality of uncontrollable organ failure) which was his escape hatch to avoid having to be with me.

A few months before, we'd talked about me moving to his location. He had 'things' to sort out first. I got fed up after a month and we never spoke again. At the funeral, I learned he was living with another girl.

I expected it to take a couple of years to recover, not 10. At first, I focused a lot on work and weekend partying, then hobbies. I'm possibly going back to uni for three years for a career change. It feels that things are finally looking up, like a real turning point.

My parents are still together, but their communication is lacking. My mom is nice but irrational and over-dramatic at times. She unfairly blames all negative occurrences in her life on my dad, while he just lets her/pretends not to hear (and immerses himself in work). I hate both sides of that coin. Can that cycle be broken?

My first real boyfriend relationship lasted for two years in high school. It was mostly a positive experience for me, but things went very wrong when he took his friend's word over mine after he sexually assaulted me. The other guys, who were actually there, were offering to testify but I dropped it and went a bit off the rails for the rest of uni.

I don't think I have a good sense of what to expect in a real, solid relationship. People say I'm too busy to meet anyone. Is it my accent? Do I have too much baggage? Is it too late for me?

Andrew writes:

It's never too late to find love, so let's hit that on the head straight-away. What's wrong with you? Nothing. You sound sensible, caring and together. Why are you single? You've had some bad luck—a mother who dumped her feelings onto you, a father who is caring but not always available and, something that you completely underplay in your letter, you were sexually abused and, worse still, let down by the person who should have believed you. I'm getting angry with him just typing this answer.

One of the problems with burying abuse is that you can be left with a nasty message: 'It was your fault.' Sadly, if left unchallenged, it will be carried over into future relationships—so you feel responsible for your 'should have married' boyfriend not fighting for his life in the ambulance. It can also make you frightened to challenge and ask questions like: what are these 'things' you need to sort out? (Men seldom mean cleaning the house or making some room in their wardrobe! It's nearly always code for being involved to some degree with someone else.)

What is particularly dangerous is when experiences in our formative dating years chime rather than heal any toxic messages from our childhood. In your case, your mother blames your father for all her problems and I expect you spend a significant amount of your energy as a kid trying to pacify her so you didn't get a bucket of blame poured over your head too!

So what can you do? Firstly, you need to change your script. Notice each time, for example at work, when you find yourself getting prickly, angry or dumped on. What's going on? Are you hearing: 'You're to blame?' Could the person simply be asking a question or just describing the problem but you've *heard* blame when none was meant? Secondly, I want you to remember my mantra: 'All problems are six of one and half a dozen of the other.' Fortunately, I think you're already some way to adopting this idea as you've found a more balanced view of your parents' marriage—for example, by understanding why your father worked so hard (rather than just labelling him as a workaholic and blaming him).

Finally, you ask: can the cycle be broken? Of course. You can learn about good solid relationships and the skills involved in making them work: asking for what you need (rather than dropping hints or expecting the other person to know), truly listening to what is being said (and stepping into the other person's shoes) and negotiating when your needs clash.

What is love? *A joint project where each partner is equally responsible for keeping it healthy.*

3. In your book *The Single Trap*, you wrote that the first step in looking for love is to work on our self. But, in recent studies (see for example the book: *Strangers To Ourselves—Discovering The Adaptive Unconscious.* T.D. Wilson, The Belknap Press of Harvard University Press: 2002) scientists have found out that

knowing our self (self-knowledge) is not easy. They are saying that our choices (for example: choosing a partner) are not only based on our conscious self but also controlled by our unconscious self. They also assert that the self consists of two parts, namely: a conscious and an unconscious. Some psychologists/therapists (see for example the book: *Couples In Collusion*. Jurg Willi, Jason Aronson: 1982) claim that our choices in fact are mostly based on our unconscious self.

My question is, if it is true that our choices (for example: choosing a partner) are mostly based on our unconscious self, how do we access this unconscious self so that we can make the right choices?

Andrew writes:

You've got it in one. Something deep inside guides us to our choice of mate—not just the good sense of humour, nice face etc. that we think are the determining factors. The secret is not so much how can we access our sub-conscious, so that we can make the right choices, but how we listen to it properly. Lots of times, when I ask someone about a guy or a woman who treated them badly, their 'better self' knew he or she was trouble but chose to ignore it. Sometimes, they were bored (and looking for distraction) or just coming out of a relationship (and needed cheering up). Sometimes, they simply let the man or woman talk them round. Whatever the reason, they ignored a little voice inside saying: beware.

So my advice is to work on yourself, so you are in a good place and will listen to your better judgement. There is another advantage of this strategy: because like attracts like and you will not only recognise other 'balanced' people but attract them into your life.

There is also an unspoken question in your letter. What is our unconscious looking for? In many ways, we're searching for someone to complement or complete us. (In my trade, this is called the 'couple fit'.) In each relationship, we need one person to raise problems (or nothing would get solved) and one person to keep a sense of proportion (or we'd always be looking at our navels). We need one person to be responsible for closeness (or there would be no relationship or intimacy) and another for separation (or we would lose our sense of self). We also need to be in touch with both our emotions and our reason in order to make wise decisions. In many couples, one partner will champion one approach and the other the opposite one.

So when looking for love, I always recommend taking away the ticking clock. On the first date, all you should consider is: do I want a second one with this woman or man? I would avoid making any decision about whether you're interested or not until the third date (or sleeping together as sex can overrule your unconscious and bind you to unsuitable people). Next, it takes about three months of dating to call each other boyfriend and girlfriend (rather than just 'seeing each other') and you don't have to decide if he or she is a keeper until about 18 months. In this way, your unconscious *and* conscious brain have enough time to know if you have found a good fit.

What is love? *Finding your other half.*

DOUBTS ABOUT BEING IN LOVE

4. I was married to a man for 27 years who had two lives. I was 47 at the time of the divorce and I tried to fix everything quickly for myself and my children by running straight into a relationship with a man who loves me but I was only thinking practically—we bought a house together. He is the kindest man and loves me very much. We share many of the same interests but I do feel like something is missing. I'm 56, and he is 62, I do not want to shake our lives up, but what I want to know is: is it possible to learn to love and be content?

Andrew writes:

You've fallen for one of the most dangerous myths about love: it should be passionate, it should sweep us off our feet and, therefore, relationships are easy and don't require any skills. It might be the case in the beginning when you are overwhelmed by your hormones and what is called limerence—but this doesn't last for ever. Fortunately, you're open to challenging the myths about love and ask: can I learn to love? Great question! I'm not certain that you can learn to love, but you can learn to communicate better, have realistic expectations and love will follow on from there.

So, where do you start? Normally, when somebody is described as 'kind' it normally means he agrees with everything you want—which is nice at a basic level but is actually rather dull. Instead of being passive (going along with what you want), your husband needs to learn to be assertive (and consider his own needs too). What this means in practice is that you can ask for something, he can say no and then you can negotiate.

The next skill you need is to know how to balance 'challenge' and 'acceptance'. We need to accept our partner, otherwise how can we love them? However, if this is a blank acceptance without any challenge it ends up being rather boring. So how could you challenge yourselves? I'd like you to put back the sexual spark into your relationship and make it more adventurous.

For example, you could try this exercise. Write down the following questions on pieces of paper, put them in a hat and take it in turns to pick one out and lead a discussion.

♥ 'What is the one thing you've never been able to tell me about sex?'

♥ 'What do you think about your body?'

♥ 'What do you like most about my body?'

♥ 'What is the most important part of love making for you?'

♥ 'How can I show you if I want sex?'

♥ 'Would sex toys improve our love making?'

♥ 'How can we make sex better?'

♥ 'Which occasion when we made sex was particularly pleasurable and why?'

♥ 'What do you wish I did more of?'

♥ 'What do you wish I did less of?'

My third idea is that you could learn about yourself and what you need, rather than expecting your husband to just know. And then we're back to assertiveness and communicating. So instead of being resentful, you can ask for those things you truly need.

What is love? *More than just the absence of problems between the two of you but feeling truly connected.*

5. I came out of a six-year relationship with my heart broken (I was 33). I moved to a new city and within five months I was into a new relationship with someone I had briefly known when I was at uni. He was kind, supportive and we had great sex and shared of lot of the same values, but I struggled constantly with trying to figure out if he was right or not, something just didn't feel right, so after two and a half years I ended it.

It's months later—I've managed to clear my head a little and realised how messed up I actually was. I was clearly not ready to get into another relationship when I did, I hadn't got over the last. I was in a new city with no friends, I had low self-esteem and I was grieving the loss of family members. I was desperate to make everything all right again and 'get some control back', settle down and have a family before it was too late (now 37). I was trying to be strong, but I should have given myself more time and learnt to love myself again.

The thing is now that I'm beginning to feel calmer, happier and stronger about myself I can't quite get this man out of my mind. I'm not sure what to do about it, I don't want to hurt him again and I don't feel totally sure about committing because I've already spent years feeling that it wasn't right.

I feel a little in limbo, not confident or sure enough to try again, but not free enough to move on and start a new search.

Andrew writes:

You're right that many people rush to 'get control' and 'feel better'—but as the majority of the problems are inside them, ending their relationship or moving to another city is not going to fundamentally change anything. Fortunately, it sounds like you've made a great start to looking at yourself and making real changes.

So what should you do? I'm often worried when people think about contacting their ex again because it's easy to mistake a natural part of the grieving process (questioning what went wrong and thinking 'what if?') for evidence that you 'belong together'. However, it sounds like you've thought deeper and longer and more importantly started to change. Therefore, I think it is worth considering contacting your ex—meeting for coffee and finding out how he's been doing. Whether he wants to give the relationship another try or not, I think it would be good for you to update him on your journey and apologise for your part in the break-up. Maybe, he will be already dating someone else or too hurt to risk another chance—if that's the case you'll be further along in healing by having a proper ending (where you can take stock and learn) rather than just walking away.

What if he is open to seeing each other again? Start by discussing: 'what could we do differently this time?' If you can come up with lots of ideas, that's a great start; if you look at each other blankly or say something like 'try harder' that's not so positive.

Finally, I fully understand your desire not to lead him along and break his heart again. So let's look at this idea of 'feeling the relationship wasn't right'. I wonder if you have fallen for the soul mates myth—that someone is so 'right' for us and that we click on such a fundamental level (same tastes, beliefs etc.) that we 'get each other' and all problems, disagreements and issues just melt away. Personally, I don't think it's possible for two people to live together without falling out. What we need is not to be 'soul mates' but have good relationships skills. If there is a problem, we can talk about it, accept any differences and work out a compromise.

My hope is that you will both decide to date and see what happens, this will give you a chance to sort out small day-to-day stuff—like choosing which movie to see in an assertive way, rather than one person demanding (being domineering) and the other backing down or pretending it doesn't matter (being passive). From these small steps something beautiful can happen.

What is love? *Learning from your mistakes and trying to put them right.*

6. I have recently started going out with a man. He is 34; I am 36. We had a bit of a bumpy start as he is very shy and this came across to me as coldness and a lack of sense of humour. However, after the first couple of dates, we seem to be clicking more and getting on better. He is starting to open up and is talking to me more freely.

He has a lot of qualities that I really like, which make me want to get to know him better. He is loyal, hard-working, gentle, honest and caring. Also, there is real sexual chemistry between us, which in my experience doesn't come along very often!

However, there are a couple of things about him that I'm finding quite trying and, because it's early days, I feel that I can't talk to him about these issues. Also, he is really sensitive and I wouldn't want him to think I am just criticising him.

There are two problems really. The first is the way he talks, which is really quite negative. I've heard him talk about work, family and friends and, each time, there always seems to be a moan involved. It's like he's focussing on the negative and seeing things in a 'glass is half empty' way. I have hinted that he would benefit from laughing at himself and situations more but it seems a real habit and I'm not sure how/if/when it will change. I'm a fun person (most of the time) and I like to have a laugh and be silly but I really haven't seen much of that in him so I'm wondering if a) he is humorous enough for me and b) whether I'll be able to get him to lighten up.

The second problem is his communication skills. I said earlier that the first couple of dates were bumpy. This was because he was so shy that he hardly spoke and I had to work on getting him to open up. Well he's doing that now but I've noticed that he doesn't really engage with what I'm saying. If I tell a story or give an opinion, he won't comment on what I've said or ask me any questions but will move straight on to something about him. Also, he doesn't seem to ask me any questions about me and my life; it's all about him.

I've been single for a long time and haven't met anyone I like for ages so I don't want to just give up on him and not work at it. But I'm not sure whether the problems I've mentioned are signs that we're not really compatible or are things that can be overcome with good communication?

Andrew writes:

My instant reaction is that you have a great potential long-term partner here. Loyal, honest and caring—it doesn't get much better. However, something is making you hold back and I wonder if it is more to do with you than him?

I wonder if you've fallen into the 'maximiser' trap. Basically, there is so much choice today we feel that, for example, we can find the perfect jeans at the lowest price—and spend hours seeking them out. This is the behaviour of a 'maximiser'. In contrast, a 'satisfyer' will find something that fits at a reasonable price and buy them. Neither is 100 per cent right, but being too far down the maximiser end can lead to dissatisfaction because even if we make a good purchase there is always that fear that somewhere there is an even better pair of jeans at a better price which will make us even happier. Although it's great to want the best, when it comes to relationships that's hard to quantify. Especially as what annoys us about other people—for example being negative—often says more about us than them. Ask yourself, why is it so important to be positive? Did you have a parent who was always complaining and you felt, as a child, not good enough? Do you *need* to hold onto positives because if you don't everything will come crashing down and your head will be full of critical voices?

Next, I would look back into your relationship past and identify the patterns. I suggest getting out a photo of each key ex and writing down a few key words. For example, 'bad boy', 'difficult mother' and 'jealous'. When you've finished, ask yourself: have I been in this situation before? have I found seemingly great guys but slowly picked them apart—until I've decided to move on? is there a pattern here? do I get cold feet? what makes me frightened?

Now onto your specific worries about this man, he is quite reserved and he can be a little pessimistic. You might be surprised but I don't think these are a handicap either. Relationships need optimism and pessimism (which he would probably call 'being realistic'). These skills can actually be complementary and make for great team work. He will spot pitfalls where you might go rushing blindly in. Meanwhile, you can make him aware of the opportunities rather than forever holding back. The problems arise when each of you becomes an exaggerated version of yourselves. The more he worries, for example, the more you try and pull him out of it—but he starts coming up with more problems (because he's worried that your feet are not on the ground). Picture a see-saw, the more you push down on your side, the more he flies up at his end (and vice versa). So how do you become more balanced? By moving into the middle, so you both don't fly up and down on the see-saw. Listen to his concerns, acknowledge when he has a fair point and then communicate your views. If he feels heard, he will be more receptive to hearing you.

So see his 'down side' as potential positives and value them. Then when you know each other better and these qualities become a real problem, he will find it easier to hear your complaint because you are criticising a behaviour that has got out of hand rather than his whole personality.

In the meantime, enjoy his company, relax and let the good times roll.

What is love? *Valuing differences rather than getting angry about them.*

7.

I am 27 and have been with my boyfriend for over a year. This is my first relationship and sexual partner. After reading *I Love You But I'm Not In Love With You*, I realise that I never experienced the limerence phase. I have spent the past year questioning my feelings and I wonder if I feel more 'affectionate regard'. I don't know if I ask myself these questions because I have never been in a relationship, or because there is really a problem. By nature, I am an analytical person and I question everything, even though I have never questioned my partner's commitment and fidelity. I don't want to quit on this. I don't want to hurt him. But I wonder if I am trying to make excuses and convince myself to love him.

Andrew writes:

I do meet people, from time-to-time, who have never experienced limerence. In many cases, it doesn't matter because they have bonded with their partner in other ways: through children, respect and friendship. However, it sounds like you've not managed to connect yet.

Many people would just say: wrong guy. But I wonder if there is something more. Especially as you've waited until your mid-twenties to have your first relationship and explore sex. My guess is that there is one of two problems. Firstly, you are very rational and spend too long in your head—while emotions and particularly love is not a head experience but something you feel. Secondly, you might be frightened of falling in love. Perhaps your mother and father had a difficult relationship and you know, first hand, how painful love can be. Therefore, you hold back because if 'I don't love, I can't be hurt'. Alternatively, your parents love was conditional (on being good or passing exams) and you don't believe you are good enough or that you deserve to be loved.

I also want to introduce you to a key idea for good relationships (and the good life in general). *Accept your feelings but challenge your thoughts.*

If you're really analytical, I wouldn't be at all surprised if you've been accepting your thoughts but challenging your feelings! So how are you going to break this pattern? I'd like you to start a feeling diary and several times a day to write down the time, what you're feeling and why. For example, '8.45: Happy—Beautiful clouds on the way to work.' Don't judge the feelings, just write them down. I ask my clients to write down at least eight a day. Be careful that you're not putting down thoughts rather than feelings—just putting 'I feel' before something doesn't make it a feeling. For example, 'I feel it's about time she bought me a coffee because I'm always treating her.' This is a belief not a feeling. The feeling could be angry, resentful or perhaps relieved.

It's important to know our feelings because they are clues about how to behave. If you feel resentful about your friend's parsimony, you probably need to say something. However, if it's angry, it might be better to wait (because it might easily come out wrong). If it is relieved, you might let it drop. Look back at the end of the week and see if there are themes and issues that you need to address.

You'll also find that your thoughts tend to drive your feelings (and either make them stronger or rationalised away). For example, if you believe: 'everybody takes advantage of me', I would ask you to *challenge* this thought. What is the evidence for 'everybody'? If you believe, 'my friend won't like me unless I buy her coffee', ask yourself 'is that really true?' or 'do I want that sort of friend?'

Ultimately, if you begin to accept your feelings, you will not only make better choices but feel more comfortable in your own skin. Who knows, you may find that you're falling in love too.

What is love? *A balance between the heart and the head.*

8.

I met my girlfriend in August 2008 (she had just turned 23 and I was 29, and she hadn't quite come out as gay). We were immediately attracted to each other, then we were inseparable for at least a year. She said that she was obsessed with me, which made me feel very comfortable about the stability of our love—that it was unbreakable. She spent months asking me when I was going to ask her to marry me, which I did after a year and a half together whilst on holiday in Cape Town. We were both over the moon and so happy.

Shortly after we came back from Africa, I had a nasty relapse of my MS and was off work for six weeks. I became depressed with life and my health, but always, Kim was my rock and my ray of sunshine. We did talk when I realised that my unhappiness was not good for us, but you have to understand that it was very hard and scary for me as I hadn't had such a nasty relapse in eight years and it undermined my confidence and self-esteem hugely. Four months later, out of the blue, she said she wanted some space and wasn't sure how she felt about our relationship any more. A couple of days later, she ended it for good.

I've been devastated as I can't understand how someone could go from wanting to spend the rest of their life with you one month, then so short a time later, to leave. For both of us, it was our first relationship with anyone, and she said that I didn't have enough emotional input, we were too different and I wasn't a happy enough person. I can see now that I was depressed and perhaps became a bit distant. I didn't bother to dress up and look nice any more. I made a complete hash of her birthday but it's not like we would fall out or argue.

I saw her twice after she moved out; I cried and sobbed, and asked for another chance, but she said she knew she'd made the right decision. Reading your book has helped me understand how relationships work, and I want to give the book to her and ask for another chance. We're quite different people, she's very girlie and loves shopping and people and I enjoy playing on my Xbox, which she hates, and want to travel, which she really doesn't want to do. I love her with all my heart and still do, but I don't know whether to continue trying to fight for us, or to try and let her go in my heart and find someone I have a lot more in common with. I'm so confused about things right now.

Do I have hope? Should I let her go?

Andrew writes:

Eighteen months is a very important moment in a relationship as this is when limerence (the crazy part of falling in love) starts to wear off and some people can think this means they're falling out of love. I was not surprised that you 'never argued' as this is a common problem with ILYB— because the real issues are suppressed (by lots of cuddles on the sofa and pretending everything's OK) rather than letting them come to the surface and be sorted.

There are some other issues at play in your case. You write that your partner was not truly out when you first met. 'Coming Out' is a long and complicated process—and despite the media talk that there's no trouble today being gay or lesbian—often fraught and painful. General homophobia can throw a couple together (which is good) but isolate them and make it harder to bring up problems in the relationship (because this is your refuge). Throw into this arena that this is your first real relationship (which means you have no roadmap to fall back onto) and the stresses can get intolerable.

You wonder whether you should find someone with more similarities. Personally, I think we need a partner with contrasting qualities (rather than a carbon copy of ourselves) as this can provide some of the things we miss. Secondly, growth comes from rubbing our rough edges off against some else's rough edges. I know our society believes that if we need to find our soul partner—an emotional twin, with whom we are so in sync that we can magically fly over any problems—but this is just a myth. Basically, show me someone who believes passionately in soul partners and more times than not he or she will be alone, bitter and angry. Real partnerships are complex, with ups and downs, good times and bad ones, but much more rewarding than one-dimensional soul partners.

However, I find that lots of gays and lesbians believe that they should have a 'fabulous' relationship—partly to show the heterosexual world that gay relationships are not doomed and partly to combat the daily doses of shame that the parents of gay children unwittingly give their off-spring for being different (and the negative messages from our culture in general). Unfortunately, no relationship can be fabulous all the time.

You finish your letter by asking: 'Do I have hope? Should I let her go?' There is certainly lots to be hopeful about. You are learning, growing and becoming a more rounded person. Well done. I think, however, you should ask a different question: 'Is she right for me?' You're ready to grow and move onto a more mature relationship with solid foundations (rather than just the high of limerence) but is she?

What is love? *A skill as well as a connection.*

9. I am 20 years old, at a high pressure university and have just ended (mutually) my first 'serious' relationship.

From the beginning, I was snappy with my boyfriend. But over-all, it was a loving, intimate and very close bond (we were insepa-rable best friends first). However, as we began our second year at university, our relationship spiralled out of control due to my own anxieties. I was constantly questioning (was he interested enough in the same things? did it matter that we had different passions? were we too different? were we too similar? was the sex passion-ate enough?). I doubted every aspect—and almost always entirely irrationally. I questioned things that no one else would. I became obsessed over whether he was 'the one'. One day I was convinced we'd marry (it always made me smile when he said we would) and the next I wasn't even sure if we were compatible.

I would also start arguments over very small things. I realised after a while that this was all partly because I was unhappy in myself, yet consistently took it out on him. I went to a counsellor but didn't find it very useful. My boyfriend was everything I could wish for— the most caring, kind, patient, understanding man I have ever met—but I was constantly out to sabotage the relationship. I saw a future with him, but it scared me and I pushed him away.

My parents are divorced and I have lived as a child in a house with an emotionally (and sometimes physically) abusive relationship. I didn't realise how dysfunctional I could make a relationship before I was in one. I lost love because I didn't know what to do— I was emotionally immature. What saddens me more is when people say 'move on', 'no use looking back' and that it's always a bad idea to get back together. We know that we can't any time soon although we both want to (we did enjoy one romantic and wonderful day in London together after we were broken up).

We are sensible, intelligent people, but we love each other. Is it really so wrong to hope that we'll be amazing together one day?

Andrew writes:

I think this has been the most amazing relationship for you. It's allowed you to get close *and* discover all your fears about relationships. Rest assured, it is very common to be terrified of letting someone in (especially after a divorce and witnessing an abusive relationship) but also desperately want to be loved and have all the hurt taken away. The good news is that you've discovered this dynamic and owned up to it when you are comparatively young. I can't tell you how many people I've counselled with the same problems but who've waited until they're 35, 45, 55 or older still to seek help.

One of the themes of my books is that we have to accept our feelings, even the ones that we don't particularly like—for example, anxiety. Partly because it is telling us something important (that might need attending to) but mainly because running away or acting out makes things worse (as you've found out). By acting out, I mean picking an argument with your boyfriend in the hope that when you make up afterwards you'll be reassured that he does truly care. This is particularly important with anxiety because it is so all pervasive. (According to a report in *Psychological Medicine* one in 13 people suffer anxiety disorders.) I find a quote from the Danish 19th century philosopher Kierkegaard helps: 'Learning to know anxiety is an adventure which every man has to affront. He, therefore, who has learned rightly to be in anxiety has learned the most important thing.' In effect, you can't escape anxiety, it's part of being human. What counts is how you respond.

If you've witnessed abuse as a child (and maybe even suffered yourself) you are going to be on high alert. However, these coping strategies from your childhood are out of date. You have far more choices today (when you're a kid you are stuck in your parents house with no car keys and no means of supporting yourself). So next time, you're feeling anxious acknowledge the feeling. 'I'm anxious and that's to be expected' (rather than getting angry with yourself). You can stop, take a few deep breaths and ask: 'Is this about today or a shadow from the past?' You can talk to the other person: 'I'm feeling anxious because...' Perhaps just admitting to the anxiety will diminish it, perhaps there is a good reason for being anxious and you can have a sensible discussion about how to deal with the problem.

Finally, by all means keep a special place in your heart for your first love, but I would much rather you used this as a spur to find a good therapist (and sort out the problems from the past) so you can have a good relationship sometime in the future. Maybe with your ex-boyfriend but more likely with someone new.

What is love? *Taking responsibility for our own stuff rather than expecting our partner to sort it out for us.*

10.

I am writing to thank you for an answer you gave me a little over a year ago, concerning whether a lukewarm relationship was good enough. Your answer made me understand something of my past relationships (one of six years and a marriage of 18 years) and look at the new one from a different perspective. And ever since that realisation, lukewarm has become warmer and warmer. My appreciation and admiration for my fiancé has grown steadily and our relationship is deeply satisfying both emotionally and sexually. Actually, I've never experienced sex as good or wild as this as I have never been able to trust anybody as much as my fiancé.

So, out of lukewarm can grow something really beautiful and I'm glad you opened my eyes to see the possibility.

Andrew writes:

Thank you so much for the update. It's really nice to hear when things work out well and it gives hope to others in a similar situation. As you've discovered, sometimes changing the way that you look at something—rather than expecting our partner to change—can be a huge breakthrough. So congratulations and all the best for the future.

Here's the original letter:

I'm a 48-year-old professional with two teenage boys. I got divorced almost three years ago because of my ex's alcoholism and depression which were affecting both my kids and my own life in a disturbing way. Now I have been dating a man seven years my senior from the beginning of April. We actually first met in February, through the Internet, and he seemed pleasant but didn't make an impact on me. He thought I wasn't interested and didn't contact me again until April; when he did I thought I should give him a second chance as one meeting and looks don't reveal every-thing about a person. He has turned out to be a nice, trustworthy and caring man and we share some common interests but there are some buts, too.

Our sex life is not totally satisfying for two reasons: I'm not keen on the way he kisses and his penis is very small. For me these things sound very shallow and I had always thought that size does-n't matter; now I know it does. He is good with his tongue and fin-gers but I miss feeling a penis inside me and getting a vaginal orgasm. I sometimes wonder if I can live like this for the rest of my life. I like him a lot and appreciate his kind personality but I don't feel terribly passionate about him. Our rhythm is also quite differ-ent: he is very slow and I'm quite fast. This morning I ate muesli, a sandwich and an egg plus drank a cup of tea and a cup of juice while he was getting down his muesli. And I'm not an extremely fast eater myself.

So is it normal to have doubts at this phase of a relationship? How would I really know if there's a chance for a long lasting, mutually fulfilling relationship? Is lukewarm enough?

Here's my original reply:

I'm struck by the difference between your last relationship—with a bad boy (your ex was an alcoholic) and your current partner who sounds really nice (but possibly too nice). When there is such a dramatic differ-ence, I normally suspect that there is a link between the problems in one relationship and the next. Let me try and explain what I mean.

My guess is that life with your ex was never dull. There was lots of drama. Where is he? What state will he be in? What's going to happen next? Living with an alcoholic can involve living on your nerves with the adrenaline pumping all the time. (Interestingly, it is easy to mistake the faster heartbeat with passion and that's why lots of women fall for bad boys.) Your impatience with your current boyfriend taking his time over breakfast makes me wonder if you have become so used to drama that ordinary life comes across as rather dull.

So I want to turn your question on its head. Not is he right for you, but are you ready for him? Have you processed all your experiences from being the partner of an addict? Have you learnt all the lessons? Consider some sessions with an addiction expert to help think through your old relationship and whether you were co-dependent (addicted to his bad behaviour or a compulsive carer etc.).

This is not to say that there is not work to do on your current relationship. Experiment with different positions for sexual intercourse where he will be able to penetrate further or bring sex toys into your love-making. Show him how you like to be kissed... for example, 'it really turns me on when you kiss me (slowly, forcibly, whatever)'. If he's good at oral sex, I'm sure he can learn to kiss in a way that feels good for you.

Finally, I think there are often doubts at three months—especially after you've been hurt. The myths about love means we can expect such a big bang that it blasts away any problems and fuses two people together in a tight embrace, forever more. However, love is seldom enough on its own. We need respect, consideration, kindness and lots of other gentler qualities too. Time and again, love is something that grows slowly from a small shoot into a large tree to shelter under.

What is love? *Patience.*

FALLING FOR THE WRONG PERSON

11. I met the man of my dreams and his beautiful fiancée. I know it seems unreasonable but I am love struck. What should I do?

Andrew writes:

Feelings are clues on how to behave, they're not instructions. Basically we need to respond with our head *and* our heart, and, although your heart is telling you you're love-struck, your head is telling you this is going to bring nothing but misery. Fortunately, if you don't feed it, your love-struckness will diminish. By feeding it, I mean meeting up with him or going to places where you know he's going to be—that's just torturing yourself. Don't try to be friends either, don't web-stalk him, listen to songs of hopeless love or watch old weepie films. When you find yourself thinking about him and sighing, push that thought out of your brain. Be ruthless, don't feed the fantasy and it will get better.

When you're single, it seems like you're never going to find the right man and when you do he's got someone else! But the secret of escaping from the single trap is not to get hung up on unavailable men and spend, sometimes, years mooning after them. If this is a pattern and you find yourself falling time and again for unavailable men, you need to understand why. In most cases, I find women alternate between hopeless attraction (often to bad boys who are unlikely to settle down) and nice guys (with whom they have no real connection). In the worst cases, they are secretly texting or sexting old lovers and never really giving the new relationship a proper chance—or address any of the day-to-day problems—because they're fantasising about the man of their 'dreams'.

So be honest with yourself and don't justify behaviours that you know are wrong. In this way, when an available man comes along you will be open for a relationship with him.

What is love? *Something that doesn't hurt.*

12. I'm 25, have a good set of friends and am a chipper person. But lately I've become a bit disenchanted.

The last guy I was seeing (only for about three months) ended things after he told me that he liked someone at his work. He said that things had been complicated with her for 'a while' and that they'd now decided to pursue a relationship. I'm not miserable about it (I did have my own doubts about the relationship) but I'm annoyed that he essentially 'hedged his bets' with me during the time we were together.

The relationship before that (which was nearly two years ago) lasted six months and was a pretty brutal breakup (for me, anyway). From the start, he said he couldn't have a girlfriend as he'd only just broken up with someone else. I should've run a mile at that point, but I didn't. I thought I could change his mind. Instead we had six months of 'not going out'. When I said I loved him, he just said to me 'I can't love you' and we broke up then and there. Ouch. About a month later he was seeing someone else.

I'm a bit of a romantic really (which is surprising seeing as I'm surrounded by a history of unhappy marriages and bitter singleness: my parents—I don't have any contact with my father; my sister, who is married to a man who really doesn't make her happy; and my other sister who is in her early forties and is bitterly resigned to never meeting a man), as I believe there is someone who'll love me for just who I am.

But disenchantment has crept in based on these last two guys, who I thought were decent people but ended up flooring me. It's a combination of feeling that I'm unworthy/unlovable (which will eventually pass, I know), mixed with a growing feeling that there aren't any nice guys out there—which I know isn't true, it's just my frustration talking.

I feel like the only way I'm going to get out of my scepticism is by meeting nice guys in a totally unromantic context but I work in an all-female office, and the friends of friends that I do meet I don't tend to click romantically with.

Do you have any advice? Thanks.

Andrew writes:

I'm not at all surprised that you're a romantic—this is a very common reaction to a parent's bitter divorce. After witnessing so much betrayal and proof that love does not always last, we need to cling tightly to the dream of happily ever after. Unfortunately, we can also expect love to ford streams, leap over mountains and make a man who was upfront and honest about being unable to fall in love to change his mind. Worse still, when love fails to meet these high expectations, we don't think there's anything wrong with our picture of love but that we are somehow unlovable! (I bet you decided that he was in love with his new girlfriend, and further beat yourself up, even though it's perfectly possible that he swapped one woman offering free sex for another.)

However, what I'm really interested in is *your* relationship (or non-relationship) with your father—who is often the template for girls' future dealings with men. I would guess from your letter that he was emotionally unavailable (or in some other way destructive) as you've just been through two relationships with men who were either recovering from another relationship or lusting after another woman (and therefore unavailable). So what would happen if you looked at your parent's relationship through fresh eyes? It is very easy to take sides—especially if your mother was weeping at the kitchen table or deliberately drew her daughters into her fights with her husband. However, nobody really knows what goes on behind closed doors in a relationship—even the children (especially as they are often not old enough to understand adult matters).

With a more balanced view of love and your father, it's perfectly possible that instead of passing over men who you meet through friends, because you don't click immediately, that you will keep an open mind and see what happens. In lots of cases, a seemingly unromantic relationship will become friends with 'feelings' and before you know it the sparks will start to fly. Love sometimes takes time to develop and that's fine because as you've found, the relationships that start with a big bang often fizzle out just as quickly.

What is love? *A slow burning fuse as well as immediate fireworks.*

13. I am currently reading *The Single Trap*—thank-you for actually 'getting' the singles thing, treating us gently and not as lesser beings! For the first time I'm seeing my situation in a context which makes sense but I have to confess that I'm struggling with an important element of moving on as set out in your book.

I'm a 42-year-old woman; attractive, successful, liked and respected. I have, however, never had a relationship even though my dearest wish was always for marriage and children. I have found myself hankering after uninterested men in lengthy flirtations and, once, an affair with a married man (given my background in a respectable Catholic family, this was a huge transgression). I know that men are attracted to me but they rarely act on it. My one chance of happiness with a kind and balanced man came 11 years ago but, even in a long-distance relationship, I felt suffocated by his warmth and unable to trust the prospect of being loved.

I pushed him away after less than three months. I now no longer have any great expectations of finding someone to share my life with and I'm realistic about the prospect of motherhood at this stage in my life.

It will probably not surprise you to learn that I have identified my father as distant (it took until his early seventies for him to be diagnosed with Aspergers Syndrome) but he also displayed destructive traits in my childhood. My mother, meanwhile, qualifies very much as a martyr although she could also be described as controlling. Both suffer chronic and debilitating physical illness which ended their working lives and turned my sister and I into carers quite young. I have seen them both use their ill-health as a weapon against each other and in some ways to control my sister and me.

My difficulty is in putting this stuff to bed so that I can get on with the life I want for myself. While I can manage my relationship with my mother (though it still often requires evasive action to prevent her taking over my life), I struggle with the concept of forgiving my father. He is now in a home with Alzheimer's and I rarely visit him. The idea of a conversation with him as you've described is impossible, and even the idea of writing him a letter is unrealistic; the lack of interest, care and concern for anyone other than himself was so engraved into his personality that I feel I would—even now—be setting myself up for yet more feelings of rejection by doing so.

I feel anger and pain even writing this e-mail. And I feel profoundly ashamed that at the age of 42 these issues should still be with me and still so raw—yet to anyone who meets me I appear pretty 'sorted'.

I feel that your book could really help me to love someone and be loved in return. But if you've any other advice you can give me to get over this blockage, I'd really appreciate hearing it!

Andrew writes:

First of all, I want to take some of the weight off your shoulders. Relationships are difficult. We're not really taught about them at school. And we're fed fairy tales and simple messages by the media. Many, if not most people, feel completely confused, overwhelmed and exhausted by relationships at some time in their lives. So please don't be annoyed with yourself for not having everything sorted at 42!

So with a little of the pressure removed... where do you go from here? If writing this letter to me released some of the pain and anger, that's good; sit down and imagine that you're going to send the next one to your father. Start with your earliest memories and move slowly through everything that's been painful or distressing. Keep going until you get to the present day. Hopefully, this story will run to several thousand words. Then put it away in a drawer for a couple of weeks and look again with fresh eyes.

Imagine that you are someone else, a good and kind friend—what would she say about the letter? Are there any mitigating circumstances— like your father's mental health issues? Read some books on the subject— I recommend *Aspergers in Love* by Maxine Aston to my clients—and get a different perspective. After all, one of the hallmarks of Aspergers is not being able to empathise with other people (or put yourself in others shoes). So if you're angry with him for a lack of interest, care or concern, that's not unlike being upset because he didn't speak Mandarin. Finally write a shorter letter to your father summarising how you felt when writing the first letter and then how you feel today. There will be differences. (I should stress these are letters for yourself—not to be sent to your father.)

I know my next request is going to be really hard. I'd like you to be able to forgive your parents—as this will help you get on with your own life. One of my favourite authors is Jeanette Winterson who has written twice about her monster of a mother. (Once fictionally in *Oranges Are Not The*

Only Fruit and once as an autobiography in *Why Be Happy When You Could Be Normal?*) When Jeanette was taken to her mother's grave, as part of a TV documentary, she said something incredibly wise: 'There are only three ways for a story to end: tragedy, revenge or forgiveness.' She had chosen forgiveness. Obviously you don't want tragedy and anyway holding onto resentment is a bit like drinking poison and expecting the other person to die.

So how do you reach forgiveness? First off, there are some myths about forgiveness that need challenging—that someone has to earn it, that if we forgive, we open ourselves up to being hurt again and that forgiveness is a feeling (which we either feel or don't). In my opinion, forgiveness is a gift to yourself (as it allows you to move on and set aside resentment) rather than for the other person—which takes away the idea of it needing to be earned. Next, just because you've forgiven your parents, does not mean that you should lower your protective shield. In this way, you can still protect yourself from further pain. Finally, forgiveness is just as much an intellectual decision as a feeling. I know this is a lot to take in but hopefully it will start a longer journey where you can begin to forgive—not just your parents but yourself too.

Although I don't want you to lower your shield with your parents, because it's needed there, I want you to experiment in situations which are non-threatening and allow someone else to see a glimpse behind the 'sorted' façade. And I do mean just a glimpse. Something so small, nobody but you would recognise it. Try and find something every day and slowly but surely open up, first to friends and then to strangers, finally to men.

What is love? *Forgiveness.*

14.

I am 33 years old and can't seem ever to settle into a relationship. I perpetually have what a friend has called 'intrigue'—i.e. there are plenty of men around, showing interest; often these interests become more than that but are always short-lived (or if not short-lived then casual/sexual over a long period of time); and are often rather traumatic in nature. Either I am attracted to men who are for some reason unavailable; or often I am attracted to 'bad boy' types who ultimately treat me horribly. It all feels a bit of a mess. Actually it seems to link into other aspects of my life which are not strikingly out of control but feel vaguely dysfunctional.

My question, I suppose, is why it all seems to be getting worse as I get older?! The men more plural, yet the relationships ever more risqué or short-lived. In many ways I am increasing in confidence and self-awareness, so I don't really understand why this doesn't seem to translate into more successful relationships. I am beginning to feel like a freak!

Andrew writes:

You are to be congratulated for spotting the patterns, realising it has something to do with you (rather than just blaming the men) and making the commitment to do something about it.

So let's look at some of the questions in your letter. Why does it get worse as I get older? Firstly, the men are probably getting older and have more 'history' to negotiate; they are more set in their ways and more dysfunctional. Secondly, it sounds like your intrigues have been a distraction (to stop you looking at the core underlying problems) and like any drug, you need stronger and bigger doses to get the same reaction.

I can assure you that you're not a freak. There are thousands of people in just the same situation—although few of them have the courage and the clear eyes with which you're approaching this problem. So ask yourself: what would happen if I stopped distracting myself with all these intrigues? My guess is that the 'vaguely dysfunctional' parts of your life would come to the fore and beg to be sorted (rather than medicated with casual sex, attention from men or the drama of falling in and out of love).

It will be painful in the short term to stare the truth in the eyes but much better in the medium to long term. That's because if you're in a healthy place, you will attract other people who're in an equally healthy place (and make a healthy relationship). If you're looking for distraction or self-medication, you'll meet others who're only looking for fun (and that's not working for you any more). Although one of the myths of love is that it will rescue us (or we can rescue other people), in reality the only person who can sort us out is ourselves.

What is love? *A mirror that shows what you need to change in your life.*

MY PARTNER DOESN'T LOVE ME ANY MORE

15. My predicament is this: I think my husband has 'I love you but I'm not in love with you' but he just doesn't know it yet. We have been married for 25 years, most of them very good. We've had a few rough spots but I have always felt that getting through these made us stronger. We have two happy children, and they have both left home this year, so we are essentially empty-nesters. We have always had a very good sex life.

Recently I feel like he is bored with me. Conversations are often limited to our kids or the home renovation we are doing. There has been virtually no sex for three months, he says he's not interested and doesn't find my body attractive any more. I have been throwing myself at him, with no luck. There's no affection or touching. At night, he just says 'good night dear'.

He always wants to change my opinion. He recently chastised me for a mistake in a condescending way. When I told him I was offended by his manner he basically said he felt it was justified. An apology was very slow in coming and was given begrudgingly after several conversations about it. In these conversations, when we talk about our relationship, he doesn't speak of love being the reason we need to work at getting along better he talks about the investment he's made over time in our marriage and how it will be wasted.

All this leads me to think that perhaps I am a bit like your old favourite slippers... nice and comfy.

That's not what I want for this next phase of our marriage. I want to get back to where we were. I don't want to keep being in this sort of limbo and feeling as bad as I feel. My question to you is... Does he have to figure this out for himself or can I start the conversation and see where that leads us? I look forward to your response.

Andrew writes:

What an interesting question! I think it is better to bring the problem into the open, rather than keeping your head down, because it is easy for an unacknowledged 'I love you but I'm not in love with you' to turn into something worse: 'I don't love you any more' and finally into 'I find someone else attractive instead!'

So how do you go about broaching the subject? Of course, you could show him my book and tell him you think that's the issue. However, I think it might be better to go to the heart of the problem. Why do we stop finding our partner attractive and why do we also start treating them dismissively and disrespectfully? My guess is that he's angry about something. That's the wall between the two of you. So ask him... are you angry with me? If he answers 'No,' explain, not just at this precise moment but over the last few months or years.

I think you'll be surprised what a tirade will come out. Try not to get upset or correct him. The key is to make him feel heard—rather than shutting up and burying stuff (which is at the heart of falling out of love). So ask more questions. When else did this happen? Can you give me more examples? In this way, you'll be acknowledging where he is and accepting all his feelings (including anger) not just the nice ones (like love). Afterwards thank him for being honest and go away and reflect. I know all this will be painful but think of it as demolishing the wall between you—brick by brick.

What you'll find is that the anger is masking a whole lot of other more complex feelings, like distress (as there's something that's eating him up), sadness and loss. It will all seem horrible, but the last emotion that's always lurking under all these nasties is HOPE.

The key is to hang in, see things from his point of view and when he feels heard, he'll be able to start to correct his exaggerations and recognise that some of his anger is not about you (rather life in general or himself but aimed at you). Finally he will be ready to listen to your side and you can begin to fix these problems. Time to swap the cosy slippers for a hard hat!

What is love? *Being brave enough to ask the tough questions.*

16. 'I love you but I'm not in love with you.' These are crushing words. I still love my wife like the plants love rain. We had some past hurts but we soldiered on. We appeared to be happy just two months ago, but this month she got an apartment, moved out and says she doesn't love me like she should, and hasn't for a long time. It makes no sense—I've done a lot of thinking and the good still outweighs the bad. She said she's getting this place so we can work on us, but it seems like she's just self-destructing everything around her. I have 10 years and two children with this woman. She doesn't feel sexually attracted to me, but I'm a decent looking guy. I have had no problem getting advances throughout our marriage but I have never given them the time of day. She is the one for me. She can say all these hurtful things to me without a tear or emotion.

Is letting her go the real way to fix us? I am lost and don't know how to help us get back what I thought we so recently had. There's this guy who is now in the picture, she says he's nothing but talks to him more than me. She compared me to him but I have a home, two degrees, and am working towards a career as a Respiratory Therapist. He has one degree, a broken leg, in a motorcycle gang, no job, lives with his parents, and a ton of medical bills from his recent accident. I am better than him in these aspects. I do affectionate, loving things for her all the time. The house is always cleaned, the kids are cared for, she gets fresh flowers when she comes home, I text and tell her I love you, but it seems to make her angry that I do these things.

She told me she doesn't want to fix us right now. I think she wants to fix her. I told her then lets work on being friends, and maybe we can grow to be lovers again, but she doesn't want to talk and doesn't even call me a friend. The word she used is 'associate'. I know there are other women out there I can pursue but I don't want to. My world has come crashing down around me and I don't know why. I don't want this to be the end but it takes two to tango and right now I'm dancing alone.

Andrew writes:

I know it is devastating to hear the words: 'I love you but I'm not in love with you.' It sounds like you're still in shock and finding it hard to step into her shoes and look back over your marriage through her eyes.

From where you stand the good outweighs the bad, but for her it's become impossible to carry on. Why could that be? You come across really strongly on the page. 'I love my wife like the plants love the rain' is possibly one of the most poetic things any man has ever written to me about his wife. My guess is that you have a BIG personality and are very articulate and convincing. The downside is that you can overwhelm other people and your wife, in particular, can feel SMALL, not heard and maybe bought off. Unfortunately, there is another downside, your confidence can turn into bragging (about lots of advances) and it could be heard as a threat (if you don't work on our marriage I'll pursue other women). To be honest, that's not going to make any woman want to come back.

Next we come to the other guy, I know it is hurtful but he is a symptom not the real problem. She has become so unhappy that she is using his attention and flattery to keep her going. So although it is easy to obsess about this man (and compare yourself with him) that will take your energy away from solving the underlying problems.

You're also falling into one of the biggest traps after someone says 'I love you but' and that's love bombing your partner and reminding them of all the good stuff. It's great to be affectionate and do nice things. However, at the moment, it seems like you are trying to magic away the problems. In her mind, she's angry and you think buying flowers will solve everything! Instead of ducking difficult moments, ask her why she's upset, listen without justifying or judging, truly understand what's going on and then you can begin to fix things. After all, she could be talking to this other man because he actually listens to her!

What is love? *Stepping into your partner's shoes and imagining every word he or she says is true.*

17.

I've been with my partner for 15 years, we are both 32. We broke up not long after my partner's parents divorced (after 29 years of marriage), then got back together five years ago and still are not married.

We've just had a baby; she is three months old and my partner said 'I do love you and our daughter but I don't know if I am in love with you.' I left to visit my sister with the baby and dog. We are now in two different provinces.

He has gone for counselling and said he will continue to do so to find out what his real problems are. He said he has been emotionally numb for a lot of years. I do love him but what should I do, should I stay by him and help him, or leave with our baby? I need guidance.

Andrew writes:

It sounds like your partner is depressed, stressed and a little lost. So, although it feels really personal when he says 'I love you but not right now', he's probably having trouble accessing all his feelings—not just love—and not just about you, but about everything.

How are you doing? It must have been a horrible shock to hear he doesn't love you—especially just three months after giving birth. So what I'm going to say next will sound a little harsh: I wonder why your first reaction was to move in with your sister—rather than staying, finding out more and seeing what can be done to resolve the situation. Is this is a regular pattern, do you act first and think second? It certainly sounds like your relationship has been full of drama.

So why has he fallen out of love now? Most guys get into this fix because they want to please their partners. They go along with what she suggests—even though they are not that keen. To do this, they swallow their needs and switch off their feelings. Eventually, they switch off all their feelings (hence the depression). It can start with something small—

like agreeing to see his wife's friends when he'd rather see his. However, it could go all the way up to agreeing to have a baby. Did you really talk about this in depth? Did he sort of agree rather than being 100 per cent up for it?

It's actually really common for men to panic about becoming fathers. While women have nine months to become mothers, men become a dad overnight. Making the adjustment from just the two of you, and the dog, to a family takes time. However, if he can't talk about his fears—in case you'll explode—he will have held it all inside and guess what's happened? He's exploded!

So why could he be finding the transition to fatherhood difficult? Perhaps he is an older or middle child and felt sidelined by a younger sibling and, because his mother's love appeared limited, he's worried that all your love might be gobbled up by the birth of your daughter. Alternatively, he might be worried about what sort of dad he will be because he didn't have much fathering himself. Maybe it's just the thought of everything your child will need over the next 20 years (and then at college and a first car...) and how he'll ever afford it that has pushed him over the edge.

So what should you do? The good news is that he's getting counselling. Have you thought of going to couple counselling, so you can both learn to express your feelings, desires and needs, say NO if you disagree with each other and then negotiate a way through? In this way, you'll both be able to communicate without the dramas.

What is love? *Something that grows as your family grows.*

18. After five years of marriage, my wife set up a therapy session. I will admit that I have been against seeking help for fear of having to open up our marriage to a stranger. Finally, my wife went herself and during her second session she asked me to come along and indicated that she wanted to spend some time apart to think. I was completely caught off guard but in hindsight, our marriage has been cracking under the surface as a result of something I have seen with other couples, which is related to the declining health of my wife's mother. She had cancer and we have been caring for her for the past two years.

Chemo every two weeks in our home took its toll and I feel that we have not had a normal marriage in the past couple of years as a result of the anticipatory grief. I would never change the love or treatment we provided her mother since it was natural. However, I cannot help but reflect how it has effected many aspects of our marriage. Financial conversations meant little to my wife since understandably everything was secondary to her mother's illness. I felt like she did not hear me lately and so I began to bottle up my feelings and treat her more coldly. The reality is that we had both been bottling up our feelings, then exploding.

Her mother just passed away; it will likely take her a long time to heal since both of her parents are now gone and she is only 38. I feel selfish wanting to mend our marriage wounds and begin to heal and am confused how I should now act. I know my wife will need time but it hurts that she does not want me around. I want to be there to help her with her pain but I know that I am more of a distraction so she asked me to only attend the wake briefly and not attend the funeral. OUCH!

I did follow her wishes, as hard as it was. I have also begun seeing the therapist that she has been seeing but they seem to imply that if people have fallen out of love then things are over. You and your book suggest to me that there might still be hope.

There has been no infidelity, no physical abuse, no alcohol or drug dependence, just little arguments that turn into big disagreements and my unhappy attitude that is the result of the past couple of years; lack of communication has led to some emotional abuse which I now look back on and regret.

I fear that more time apart without communicating with my wife is hurting our chances of reconciling. However, I realise that my wife has to grieve and reflect upon her mother's passing first before we move on and tackle our marital strains. Am I answering my own question here? I am just scared that the therapist is imply-ing that our love cannot be rekindled.

Andrew writes:

Congratulations on taking such a thoughtful approach to this prob-lem. You are right 'I don't love you any more' and bereavement often go hand-in-hand. There is nothing that makes us more aware that our time on earth is finite than sitting at a parent's deathbed. And if we're not going to live forever then we certainly don't want some half life of rows, coldness and sulks. But how horrible, to be asked not to come to the funeral! Your wife has become an orphan in her thirties and her reaction is to exclude rather than to reach out for your support. (I've just let out a big sigh as I type this reply.)

So what should you do? The most important thing to stress is don't panic. Many people end up pushing their partner out of the door by trying to fix the problem immediately (or at least by the weekend) and end up going 'yes but...' to the problems or not really listening because they're booking a second honeymoon. In your case, this is going to take longer than most to turn round. Your wife needs time to grieve, and pushing your marriage problems to the top of the agenda would be insensitive. However, I'm worried that she might interpret your respectful distance as lack of caring. If it is possible to talk with her, I would apologise for your mistakes over her mother's illness. List all the things that you regret— without an explanation as this can sound like justification and limit the impact of the apology. (As US President Benjamin Franklin famously said: 'Never ruin an apology with an excuse.') I call this a Fulsome Apol-ogy because it acknowledges regrets and the impact on the other person—

rather than just 'sorry' over and over again. Don't follow up with a request to try again or an explanation of how to solve the problem—as it'll sound like you're apologising as a means to an end. Just let your apology stand on its own. If she doesn't say anything, give her time to reflect and then walk away.

Next, think of some caring actions that a friend might offer to lighten her load. After a bereavement, there's a million things to do—like emptying your mother-in-law's house or going through piles of paperwork. How could you help? Stress you are not going to talk about your relationship or the future, but be supportive in a practical way. This kind of solicitous behaviour will show that you love her and make her realise that you can be a port in a storm.

When you are friends again and the first three months have passed after the funeral, that might be the moment to talk about the future. In the meantime, travel optimistically, don't keep looking for reassurance (as this will push her away) and learn to like each other again.

Incidentally, I would think about seeing your own therapist—rather than your wife's—as when you've got such different agendas it is hard for one counsellor to support both halves of the relationship. So find someone who will listen to you, make you feel heard, rather than just a client's significant other.

What is love? *Love is effort with both partners regularly and routinely attending to each other's needs—no matter how they feel at the time.*

19. I was in a two-year relationship. My boyfriend loved me madly and deeply, and if anything I had more doubts than him at points. The truth is, we spent every waking hour together and barely argued. It was perfect. He woke up one day and all his feelings were gone. He felt so awful, but told me because he couldn't bear to keep it from me and being with me didn't feel right. He said it was something in his gut, and he just felt different when he was with me.

He has diabetes and suffers often from periods of depression and anxiety. It has always been like this, but the one thing he always held onto during these episodes was me and my support. Before we broke up he had been having a life crisis, rethinking everything yet still centering his life and future around our relationship. The feeling of 'love' left involuntarily one day, like a switch went off.

Is there hope? Is it possible that his subconscious shut something off? I will do all I can to be here and understand. But I wish there were a better way of knowing whether this 'hope' I have is an illusion.

Andrew writes:

When you're depressed, you need something really strong to burst its way through the background greyness. When you're anxious, you need a constant boost to block out your fears. For lots of people, that's love with a capital L. The sort that is so overpowering that you want to do nothing but be together and if that's not possible, to bore your friends about each other. The sort of love that you shout from the hills and pop song writers tell us is the 'Wind beneath my wings'. With this kind of love, you can face anything.

Unfortunately, the 'crazy, walking on air, can't live with you' elements of love peak between six and 18 months into a relationship. It's no reflection on the quality of your love. Limerence simply does not last forever. In fact, scientists have tracked the chemicals that we associate with these almost addictive qualities of love in the brain—dopamine, oxytocin and phenylothylamine—and found they begin to fade around the same time. So I can quite understand how your boyfriend could feel that a switch has been flicked—especially if he's been relying on limerence to hold all his personal demons at bay.

Sadly once limerence wanes lots of people think they're not really 'soul' mates and move onto the next relationship and the next, always hoping to find that elusive forever. Most people, however, use limerence as nature intended: to bond us enough to set off on a lifetime's journey together (because without the confidence boost and the sense of 'you and me against the world' who would hitch their future to a complete stranger?).

At this point, love moves into what I call 'Loving Attachment' which unlike limerence needs skills, the ability to compromise and to accept each other in all our complexity—rather than being blind to each other's failings. As you can imagine, we also need to be able to argue constructively without burying issues; one person steamrollering over the other; getting personal or escalating the argument (so what starts as a row over where to keep the bin bags becomes about the future of the whole relationship). People also stop spending 'every waking minute together'—because they learn to be two individuals again as well as a couple.

So is there any hope? I think there's bucket loads. However, you will need a more realistic view of love. If you didn't learn to argue properly as a child then watch what works for your friends and emulate them. (I also have several books that will help too, see Further Reading.) Your boyfriend needs to face his demons and understand why he is depressed and anxious. My guess is it will be something about his childhood. So he might like to speak to his doctor about getting some counselling (CBT and Mindfulness have both been proved helpful) or consider medication.

What is love? *Something that evolves and changes.*

THE SPARK WENT OUT

20. My husband left me three weeks ago as he was unhappy in our marriage. This has devastated me as I only knew something was wrong a few weeks ago when he became quite distant (no one else is involved). He said he still loved and cared about me but that the spark was gone, also he didn't fancy me any more and our love life had become routine, as had our life together. He also said (and I think this is a major point) that I had lost my motivation and drive and I wasn't the person he had married.

We have talked a lot (and had an introductory counselling session at Relate) but at the moment he doesn't know whether to completely call it a day or try again—he is worried about trying again in case things slip back to how they were and he has to hurt me all over again.

I have already begun to change (the whole situation made me take a long look at myself) and I've started to see old friends and get started on sorting myself out, but I desperately want him back to give our marriage another chance. Do you think there's hope for us and what sort of things should I expect from my husband in the coming days and weeks? I'm so unhappy at the moment but trying to give him space and not pressurise him.

Andrew writes:

I definitely think there is hope, especially as it seems that you have the courage and self-belief not to pressurise your husband. (Many people turn a difficult situation into a crisis by pushing for an answer—which makes most men decide to end the relationship once and for all.)

What should you expect from your husband over the next few weeks? Firstly, he will blow hot and cold. When you step back and carry on with your life, he will be interested and available. When you become keen, he will run away again. So what's going on in his mind? Firstly, somewhere in his heart, he will want to make this work—otherwise he wouldn't have gone to Relate. However, he is frightened of leading you on (and upsetting you all over again). Secondly, he is frightened that you'll think that 'working on the relationship' means it will work out and that once the 'trying harder' phase is over that you'll slip back into the old ways again (and he'll be stuck there forever).

I also think there is an important topic missing from your letter: SEX. OK you skirt round the subject and talk about your love life getting 'routine' but your main prescription seems to be go out more with friends. There seems no detailed examination of what has gone wrong in your sex life. Meanwhile, your husband is talking in code too. When men talk about the 'spark' going out of their relationship, they mean that their sex life is about as interesting as cold porridge. In their mind, they think saying 'the spark has gone' sounds like a reason that blames neither partner. However, it just leaves couples feeling helpless and hopeless.

Let's look at the rest of his code, he says you've lost your 'motivation and drive' (what he means is that you don't seem to fancy him any more) and you're 'not the woman he married' (let me translate, you used to fancy him). Guess what happens if you think someone is going through the motions in bed, not really interested in you and ticking boxes. Yes, you're right. You close yourself off to avoid the hurt and disappointment. It works but only up to a point. You feel distant, sex is less satisfying and hey presto: you've lost the spark.

In an ideal world, he would have talked to you ages ago, rather than waiting till he fears your spark is past rekindling. Staying with my ideal world, everybody would also take responsibility for their own desire—rather than expecting their partner to spark it up. Couples would learn how to bridge from the everyday world of earning a living, running a house and bringing up children into the sensual world of love-making—rather than just relying on lust alone (as we do at the beginning of a relationship). But I suppose if we lived in that ideal world, the polar ice caps wouldn't be melting and chocolate wouldn't make us fat!

So how do you save your marriage? You need to show him by your actions—not just your words—that his leaving has been a huge wake up call.

1. You have truly changed (rather than just appeasing him).

2. You believe that real changes need to be made in your sex life. For example, you'll need to understand what turns you on, learn to express your sexuality and realise that if you seldom initiate it leaves all the responsibility on his shoulders.

3. Working at your marriage comes with no preconditions. If things don't work out, you will not be angry and let down but able to move on knowing you've done your best.

Good luck.

What is love? *Making sex a priority.*

21. Thank you for your clarity in *I Love You But I'm Not in Love With You*. After 15 years and three young children, my husband dropped the ILYB bomb on me eight months ago. Since then, he can neither bring himself to leave me or work on improving our relationship. He has always been a wonderful friend, husband and father. I am the first to admit that our kids came first and we didn't have outside help raising our children. Making the children our priority and exhausting ourselves has come at a huge price. My feelings for my husband are, and have been, deep and true. He no longer feels the 'spark' for me and says we have grown apart. There isn't anyone else involved. As in your book, his moment of clarity came after his father passed away.

I have made positive steps to put our relationship first, for example arranging sitters for the children. But none of it seems to resonate with my husband. He is stuck, deciding between the lesser of two bad decisions: staying with me or hurting our kids. All he sees is gloom. He talks to me politely, but he is detached and there is no affection. I initiate intimacy, he doesn't. He drinks a lot now as well. I've suggested he see his doctor but he refuses.

Andrew writes:

Congratulations for owning up to one of our society's worst sins: putting the children first. It is so widespread that if I ever challenge it, people look at me as if I'm a monster. 'Of course, we should put our children first.' 'It's only right to want the best for them.' 'We don't want them to slip behind. It's a competitive world out there.' All these knee jerk reactions... but as you've discovered, making children the priority comes at a cost. Our partner feels neglected. We are exhausted and snappy. And do the children really benefit that much? They need to learn to take responsibility themselves rather than expect their parents to always roll out the red carpet.

If you haven't apologised already to your husband, please do so. Next, imagine that your husband is now your number one priority. Think through your day, how would it be different if that was truly the case? For example: would you stop what you were doing when he came home and give him a couple of minutes of your attention (like you do for the children)? Would you come back early sometimes from a class or fun night out because you haven't spent much time together? Create good habits and follow through—rather than making grand gestures like getting sitters. (This can be seen as buying someone off and once he's back in the pen again, you'll return to normal.)

Next, let's return to ILYB. All the research into why men fall out of love points to their lack of assertiveness (i.e. not being able to ask for what they want or need). So look at your relationship through fresh eyes. 'Do I really listen to him about household issues?' Returning to the children again, a mother is in an incredibly powerful position. Nobody questions what she says—from what time to feed children, to bed times and upwards. Many times, men are not equal partners bringing up their children but assistants (and sometimes ones without a voice). No wonder they switch off and detach, even though they love their kids. This is just a hunch but ask for his advice, stop being Chairman of the Board and listen to what he has to say. Maybe even share some responsibility. In this way, you won't be so exhausted and probably up for sex a little more often...

Which brings me onto the next point. Men use sex to get close but women have to feel close to want sex. I can't tell you how many marriages have collapsed because neither side understands this central truth. Sadly, it's incredibly difficult to talk candidly about sex without having a row. While if we fancy going somewhere different on holiday, we'd tell our partner and research different possibilities together. Just asking 'can we talk about our sex life' is likely to be met with 'what's wrong with it?' or 'are you having an affair?' So we tend to struggle on doing what worked 10 or 15 years ago. We're not wearing the same style of clothes or going to the same restaurant as when we first met, but we're still having the same sex. No wonder many couples lose their spark!

You can turn your love life around by using a technique called 'Appreciative Enquiry'. Normally, we focus on problems to find a solution. However, when it comes to talking about sex this can be extremely destructive. We become defensive and that makes us less creative. Listing everything that's wrong can also make us feel helpless and hopeless.

Appreciative Enquiry turns this on the head by concentrating on what's working or what used to work. As the name also suggests, it is based on asking questions. 'When was our sex life good?' 'What made it good?'

'What, in particular, did you like?' 'How could we get more of that into our lives again?'

The next stage is to *dream* about how you'd both like sex to be. So ask questions again like: 'What would be ideal sex?' 'What would you like to try that you've not been able to tell me before?'

Finally, you *design* your new sex life: 'How could we turn this aspiration into a reality?' or 'What resources have we got that will help?' (For example, more time now the children are older and the money for a dirty weekend away.)

If any negatives comes up during Appreciative Enquiry, write them down (so they can be addressed on another occasion) and then return to talking about positives: what promotes good sex and your aspirations for the future.

Finally, you ask in your letter: how long can I live like this? Hopefully much longer if you start to empower yourself. Your new plan is to put your husband first, make him an equal partner in the decisions about the children, listen to him and carefully consider his opinions and revisit your sex lives together. Of course, it will take time to turn things round but you have been brave and caught the problem early.

What is love? *Listening to what your partner has to say— even if it is upsetting—without cross complaining, getting defensive or shutting down.*

22. I have been with my wife for about 10 years, married for the last four. Following the birth of our child three years ago it did become more difficult to find quality time for each other and our sex life was very intermittent at best. However, since late last year my wife seemed to start shutting me out of her world, rarely showing any interest in even discussing our days at work or anything much at all. Our sex life died completely with my wife mentioning body image issues (I have always been clear that I'm attracted to her) and lack of interest in 'that kind of thing' whenever I have attempted to initiate any form of intimate contact.

Early this year, my wife was diagnosed with depression. I asked her what I could do to help but didn't really get much in the way of a response. Despite this, I made an effort to stay positive, not to moan or start arguments about things that really don't matter in the grand scheme of things. I have done my best to give her the time to herself she said she needed. Nothing I tried to do for her seemed to help or even get much acknowledgement and I ended up feeling increasingly lonely and unloved. I tried to maintain a brave face; knowing it was never going to be an easy ride but hoping that over time things would improve if I didn't give up.

Some weeks ago when my wife was using her computer I noticed that her pattern of typing made it seem as if she was chatting with someone. Unsure of whether I was being paranoid or not, I examined her laptop while she was out one day. What I found shocked me and felt like being run over by a bus. My wife has been having very explicit sex chats with a number of men for the best part of a year. On most days, when she has been alone in the house, she has been having video chats where it would seem neither participant in the conversation has left much to the imagination. If there was a bright side to be found, it would be that my wife does have some interest in sex after all, apparently just not with me.

I initiated a conversation where I explained that I felt she was shutting me out of her life and that I suspected she had found more interesting people to converse with online. My wife responded with an ILYB explanation and downplayed the internet chatting as 'having had a few chats but nothing serious'. We agreed to try to find a way to work through our problems but there is an undercurrent because her view is that we have lost our 'spark' and that there is no 'passion' and it may well be irreversible. I truly hope it isn't, more than anything I want a full relationship with my wife back.

I've bought the *I Love You But I'm Not In Love With You* book and we are both reading our way through it—the book has offered a valuable insight into what we've probably both been doing to each other for too long. However, the lack of 'spark/passion' topic is present whenever we talk about how we think we're doing. This feels like a chicken and egg problem—there is not going to be much sparking or passion when the level of intimate contact has been zero for so long, but without a spark how do we manage to start getting intimate again?

Andrew writes:

First of all, let me reassure you it is possible to get the spark back into a marriage.

I think the place to start is with the depression. In most cases, depression = suppression. In other words, she is keeping back feelings for fear of upsetting you (and other people). In most cases, this is anger. Does she feel that she's the 'in charge' parent and you're just 'helping out'? Having a child is wonderful but it's not always what you imagined and there's a lot of complex stuff from your own childhood that comes up. Sometimes the depressed person is angry with themselves. Some mothers feel they are not good enough. Others discover that babies bring as many losses (like freedom) as there are gains. Unfortunately our society frowns on such ideas as selfish. As you can imagine, these feelings of guilt, shame or anger are tough to deal with and we'd much rather run away (and suppress them). If any of this rings bells, I think it would be really helpful for your wife to find someone to talk to about her depression.

In many ways, my advice to get the spark back is not so much about encouraging good times (in the hope of generating intimacy) but removing any obstacles that's stopping it coming through. So instead of focusing on more positive interactions (which helps but as you've found is not enough), I think you've got to be prepared to listen to her anger and unhappiness.

I know this is tough and you'd much rather be arranging dates (the nice bits of marriage) rather than facing up to problems (the nasty bits). It is also going to need time and patience to turn this round. However, when you've stopped adding to the wall between the two of you (and taken away the bricks of anger), you will be ready to get the spark back.

What is love? *Facing the negatives without fleeing or trying to impose a quick fix.*

23. I am stuck in a horrible cycle with my wife of 22 years that just never resolves itself. On the surface I put a lot of effort into our relationship—I listen and am attentive, generally give my wife the freedom to do what she wants to do and encourage her, try to be collaborative, focus on her pleasure during love making and keep myself active and fit and intellectually sharp.

However, beneath the surface I continually resent her because she rarely reciprocates, is a bit of a control freak and quite lazy. I am always approaching this with the wrong motivation, as if by ticking all the boxes on the 'perfect husband' scorecard that my resentment towards her is somehow justified and/or that she will 'see the light' and change.

My big mistake was marrying when I wasn't in love, but for ideological reasons because I was critical of our society's ability to commit. A few years ago, I really fell in love with someone else but didn't have an affair except inside of my head. These paradoxically were my most productive years but also triggered a near divorce and a nervous breakdown.

So, with that behind me, and with a family I love and want to keep together where do I go from here? My wife and I seem eternally wary of each other.

Andrew writes:

Oh dear. What a horrible muddle. A decent and principled man who has somehow ended up hurting himself and everybody around him.

I'm not surprised that your wife is wary of you, holds back and sounds rather angry beneath the surface. I've counselled lots of couples where there is an unspoken secret—or an accusation that is occasionally thrown but vigorously denied. It eats away at the heart of the relationship despite everybody's determination to be nice and keep the show on the road.

Let me try and put you into your wife's shoes. At some deep level, she knows that you don't love her. Can you imagine how that makes someone feel about themselves? She could also be angry about your affair 'in your head'. Although you didn't cross the line into sexual betrayal, it probably involved some sort of emotional betrayal. I would be surprised if your wife didn't register, on some level, your absence from your marriage. Therefore, she could be protecting herself from further hurts.

So what are you going to do about this?

If you were seeing me, I would try four different paths:

1. *Discover if you have had an idealistic and unreasonable idea about love.* We get a lot of our ideas about love from Hollywood movies and the idea of soul partners where being 'meant' for each other and connecting on such a deep level means that it can magic away any problem. As you can guess, this is impossible and stops us learning the necessary skills to make a relationship work. Returning to the affair in your head, by its very nature, this is going to be based on fantasy, suppressed lust and special moments snatched together. If you're basing what love means on this explosive mix, you are likely to be disappointed by the day-to-day reality.

2. *Stop suppressing your feelings.* It starts with your anger and resentment but, over time, it will become all your feelings. Even the tender ones and, dare I say it, the loving ones. If you are honest with your wife, let your anger out about her being a control freak and lazy, you will slowly but surely get in touch with *all* your feelings and not just the negative ones.

3. *Tell the truth and shame the devil.* It will be horrible but there is an opportunity to change. She gets all her anger out. She discovers about the affair in your head (assuming she doesn't already know) and can begin to deal with her lack of trust for you. I think it goes without saying that you would probably need to be in relationship counselling to achieve this but once the dust has settled you can look at the REAL truth. My guess is that you did love your wife. I doubt you would have got married just to prove a point. It's just that you went into this relationship without the soul mate 'can't live without you' kind of love. (And ultimately, it doesn't matter because you've got something more valuable: a 'raising a great family and getting through all these problems together' kind of love.) Furthermore, once these secrets are said out loud, in the real world, they can be tested. Most people find that they did love their partner but the delicate buds of early love were squashed by their fears of being hurt.

4. *Ignite a spark between you.* Sometimes touch is stronger than a thousand words, so I would finish by putting you on a programme of sensual touch. (It starts with stroking and non-genital touching and slowly builds up the levels of sexual intimacy over several weeks.) There is nothing more healing than plenty of hugs and close physical contact really can help couples start afresh.

What is love? *Trusting our partner is strong enough to cope with the truth.*

24. I've been in a relationship for eight years with a creative, smart and caring guy. Sometimes I think he's too good for me, and just seems too nice. We recently got engaged and are in the process of flat hunting and planning our wedding, but at times I have my doubts, as I have done on and off throughout our relationship. We rarely have sex and I just don't know if we are friends rather than lovers. The reason for not having sex is down to me, I do not fancy my fiancé enough and find the whole thing awkward. I know this upsets him.

We have similar interests and do get on really well, I work away a lot for months at a time and he's very supportive. I think we bring out the best in each other at times but just can't put my finger on what our relationship is missing or the next step to take. I do find myself attracted to other guys. I think I'd like children which my partner does too but my job is really important to me and it scares me knowing that I would lose that. I also don't feel my parents demonstrated a particularly 'happy' marriage environment so I don't know if that is something making me feel trapped.

I did have a sort of fling last year when I was away with work. We just kissed but didn't sleep together. Sometimes I ask myself could I get married to my partner but just have affairs? Which I know is probably not healthy...

Andrew writes:

This is a really honest letter and that's good because instead of swirling round in your head, it's all down in black and white and we can see what's really going on. You've also identified the nub of the problem: you're frightened of repeating your parent's mistakes. However, at the same time, you desperately want to be loved and start a family. So how do you reconcile these conflicting emotions?

It's something I see all the time—you have split off love from sex. So you have an emotional connection with your fiancé but fancy someone else. In this way, it seems safer because all your emotional eggs are not in the same basket. However, as you've spotted, this solution does not breed lasting happiness and affairs make everything a million times worse.

There is probably another part of the problem. He's so nice that he doesn't kick up a fuss about the disappearing sex life. In the meantime, you're avoiding the issue too. In fact, I bet you are both good at squashing down conflict, agreeing to differ and forgetting problems. However, having no arguments is a prime reason for the sexual spark going out—as tension, not knowing what's coming next, someone being their own person (rather than your possession) and rubbing off each other's rough edges all breed excitement, passion and desire.

Next, I'd like you to look if you are unconsciously turning yourself off. Do you wear your partner's old baggy T-shirts to bed? When it seems that you're getting close—like cuddling on a sofa during a romantic movie on the TV—do you suddenly remember that the tumble drier needs emptying and leap up? Do you use other distancing tactics—like reminding yourself of his nasty habits and bits of his body you consider unsightly or obsess about your own figure and imagine he can't really love you because, for example, you've got sticking out elbows? Recognising these tactics that undermine your relationship and catching them before they get established in your head will also make a major contribution to igniting the spark.

Finally, I'd like to challenge something in your letter. If your job is important to you, why do you have to give it up to have children? Lots of mothers continue to work! You could be one of them.

So summing up, I hope that reading about how you got into this mess, talking to your fiancé about your disappearing sex life (rather than letting it be an unmentionable subject) will help you find a way forward. But whatever you do, don't get married and have affairs. It will bring nothing but misery to you and your partner.

What is love? *Allowing yourself to be vulnerable enough to become close both emotionally and physically.*

25.

My boyfriend doesn't feel sexually attracted to me any more. We have been together for four years, he is 32, I am 29. We met when we were both living abroad (I am Dutch, he is English) and fell very much in love. Since then our relationship has been the opposite of standard. From long-distance to living together in 10 square metres. He broke up with me a little less than two years ago after I found out he had had very intense contact over skype/chat with his ex while I was away travelling. It was only then that I found out how unhappy he had been and how much he had disliked living in a tiny space together. The months previously I had only observed that his sexual appetite was much less than it used to be (we used to not be able to get enough of each other). Our break-up lasted about eight months. In this period he secretly went to visit his ex and lied to me about seeing another woman. Although we were not officially together, it left me really heartbroken and depressed, and above all it shattered my trust. I had emotional problems (I started seeing a counsellor), had panic attacks and was not really able to be on my own. Later my boyfriend told me he felt he had to take care of a little girl.

We got back together a little over a year ago. The first months we had many fights, and I had a million questions. I struggled with trust (felt his ex was still a threat), continually asked for reassurance of his love and felt very insecure. Also, I frequently got angry, but mostly very upset, especially when it came to my boyfriend wanting things for himself, like spending some time alone, or when he did not say the things I wanted to hear. I have to say that I really disliked the person that I had become, I was always very independent and strong, that seemed to have evaporated completely. Meanwhile, my boyfriend was really accommodating and did a lot of the things I wanted or asked for (probably out of guilt for what had happened). Despite this, it never seemed enough and often I did not respect what my boyfriend asked for. For example, I just rocked up at his house unannounced or would get really upset when he didn't pick up his phone.

The last eight months things have been much more steady. We seem to resolve arguments and communicate more effectively. I am feeling better myself and (even though I do not always like it) respect the 'space' my boyfriend asks for. I have been able to listen and not get upset or angry so easily any more. Furthermore, my trust is building up (but I do still struggle with this) and I am becoming my old (confident) self again. My boyfriend has also talked much more freely and openly about how he feels and what he wants. This made me realise that, in the past, he often did things to please me or others and not so much to please himself.

However, the most important struggle we face is in the bedroom. Since we got back together, sex has become more infrequent, and we haven't had any sex in the past five months. Although my boyfriend says he loves me and finds me very beautiful, he tells me he has absolutely no desire. Since he is not happy and misses the sex and the attraction for me, he also feels he is not ready for any further commitment (like moving in together again, something I would really like) and doubts the relationship as a whole. On the other hand he does not want to throw things away. We talked about what we liked and what we disliked about each other, and it became clear to me that he feels I am not the self-confident woman he fell in love with. Could that be a clue for his lack of sexual interest in me?

I really don't know what to do any more, nor does my boyfriend, we feel quite stuck. What can I do (and what can he do) in order for my boyfriend to feel sexually attracted to me again (and for the relationship to get its spark back)?

Andrew writes:

I am not surprised that you're feeling stuck as problem has piled on top of problem (the ex-girlfriend, splitting up, lack of trust, insecurity etc.), none of them has been properly resolved and you're both completely overwhelmed. However, your letter is full of personal insight and an ability to look honestly at yourself—that's something to be really proud about. I hope it will be the beginning of your fight back.

So let me explain what's been going on and how to get the spark back sexually. Men are trained to act rather than listen to their feelings (which they hope will go away if they put their head down). Meanwhile, they are socialised to play great store by their sex life (it's how they get close and fulfil their needs for intimacy). In effect, they ignore their heart and listen to their penis. Unsurprisingly, problems that are not necessarily sexual come to light in the bedroom. In effect, if his penis goes limp, he suddenly pays a lot of attention. He might think 'ahhh I don't fancy my wife or girlfriend' but actually more times than not he's angry with her and that's why his penis won't respond. (After all, it's made of flesh and blood not the machine that most men imagine.)

So why is he so angry? Before I explain more, you have to realise that men find women's anger incredibly hard to process (so shut down, run away or appease). Your letter is full of clues to why he's been appeasing you—even though he's furious inside. You don't respect what he wants and just 'rock up' at his apartment. When he wants something for himself you get angry (although for perfectly good reasons) so he shuts down because he's guilty and thinks he's lost the right to what he wants (because he's been unfaithful). Furthermore, if he says something you don't like, guess what, you get angry! However, instead of getting angry back, he turns it into resentment, frustration and buried rage.

There is another problem running alongside this merry-go-round. Well done for spotting that your lack of self-confidence is part of the problem (beyond making you controlling and him angry). Most men take responsibility for initiating sex. I can't tell you what a huge burden this can be on them and more importantly their penises. Unless we feel 100 per cent confident of delivering a rock hard erection—and satisfying our woman—we stay on our side of the bed. That's because the humiliation of not being able to deliver is so high that we almost feel we're not a man at all. Truly, the stakes are that high! If our partner dislikes her body and has zero confidence, she is not going to feel sexy. If she's not feeling sexy, she is giving her partner no fuel to get his engine going—in effect he's on his own and has to spark himself. OK, he can do it with a bit of fantasy but if he's also angry and thinking 'she doesn't fancy me any way' it becomes almost impossible to get the show on the road.

What needs to be done? Obviously, your partner needs to learn to be more assertive (speak up for what he needs rather than always backing down), learn to listen to his feelings (rather than bury them) and realise sex is not all up to him (it's a joint responsibility). I wish all men would also realise that erections come and go (if you don't worry, they do return) and they have tongues and fingers which are actually far better at giving women orgasms than penises! Meanwhile, I'd like you to take more responsibility for your self-esteem rather than expecting your partner to boost it up by dancing attendance all the time.

So what can you do? Walk away when your friends are bonding over who hates their body the most or how fat their thighs are. Cut down your social media consumption dramatically as much of Facebook etc. is people showing how wonderful their skiing holiday was, how cute their kids are and oh 'I have such a wonderful life'. Research has linked time spent on-line with increases in anxiety and depression. Limit yourself to an hour or even better half an hour a day. Next, find a sport or active hobby (like cycling or hiking) that will get you hot and sweaty (so you're less worried about how your body looks) rather than just going to the gym (which gets you comparing yourself with others and being self-critical). Not only does sport produce feel good hormones, it takes you out of yourself and helps you feel part of something bigger. In a similar vein, volunteer for something—like helping kids or old people—as it will pro-mote feeling capable and worthwhile too. Finally, find out more about affairs, and understand why people are unfaithful rather than assuming it was all down to you.

What is love? *Something we have to give ourself as well as our partner.*

I LOVE YOU BUT I'M NOT IN LOVE WITH YOU

26.
My wife and I have been together for the past 15 years, although we married only three years ago. I consider we are soul mates. We have fun together, we like to do the same kind of stuff and sex is great, but somehow, somewhere along the way, I started to feel I loved her in a honest and caring way, but something was missing… deep inside of me I didn't feel I was IN LOVE with her. This has been very painful and I tried to live with these feelings in silence, hoping that in time they would change, but they haven't. By the way, we don't have any children… we waited to look for a child, and when we started looking for one it didn't come.

During the past couple of years, I've lived with the struggle of either focusing on the aspects of our relationship that did work or facing the fact that I was not deeply in love (as she was, and has been all these years), and that we both deserve another relationship (especially if we were looking for a child).

This has come out in the open. She has been aware of these mixed feelings of mine, but thinks I am confused right now. We had therapy and today we are apart. I miss her very much and I wonder how can I possibly have so many things in common, have a strong sexual attraction and yet not feel in love?

Andrew writes:

You are great friends *and* the sex works too. It's tough to understand what the problem might be. However, I have two sets of totally contradictory thoughts. The first is that being SOUL MATES might be the problem. The idea that two people get each other on such a deep level that all differences melt away and all problems are resolved sounds wonderful—

but it's impossible for two people to live together without falling out, wanting different things and arguing. What we need to be is not soul mates but to have the skills to sort out our differences, tell our partner difficult stuff, argue and resolve the issues. Have you been so worried about rocking the boat that you've been editing yourself and your feelings?

My other thought is that not being able to have children together is a big issue. How much have you really talked about this? I don't mean the odd hour here or there? I mean being really honest with yourself about all your feelings about children—rather than editing them so they will be acceptable to your partner. It's also important to listen to what your partner has to say, ask questions and drill down into what she's really feeling. As you can imagine, this will take time.

I talk a lot about being assertive—which I describe as 'I can ask (for children), you can say no (I can't have them) and we can negotiate' (egg or sperm donation, surrogates, adoption, fostering or deciding to be childless). Unfortunately, it is difficult to ask (as we're frightened of being turned down and would rather drop hints or hope our soul mate will somehow just know) and difficult to say no (because we're frightened that we won't be loved if we don't agree or believe soul mates *should* go along with what their partner wants) and it's really hard to negotiate (because we don't know how or haven't had much practice).

As I think the problem is little or no negotiation, let me give you my best tip on this topic. In order to get an outcome that works for both parties, you need to go through three stages:

1. Explore

2. Understand

3. Action

Unfortunately most people find uncertainty difficult and head straight for the exit by trying to impose a solution. Basically, they bypass exploring and understanding and focus in on action. To give you a rough idea, I recommend spending 75 per cent of your time exploring, 20 per cent on understanding and just 5 per cent on action.

Sadly, there are some topics where it is impossible to find a middle way or the issue is so important that there is no suitable trade (by which I mean, you can have x if I have y). I hope that 'to have or not have children' doesn't fall into this category for you but if it does, at least you will have had a proper discussion rather than deciding your future on assumptions and half conversations.

What is love? *Taking time to explore a problem and really understand where both of you are coming from before trying to find a solution.*

27. I've recently lost my 'love' for my boyfriend and it's been extremely upsetting to me. I miss those feelings so much, and it's been so hard on him because he knows I'm in a different place emotionally.

We have a long distance relationship (he's English, I'm Australian) and we've been very happy together for quite some months now. Recently he came to visit and that's when I started to feel a change in me. I began to notice that I couldn't reciprocate, and I couldn't connect with him and feel that same bond that we had before.

I have some indicators that might have triggered the change. During our time apart, I would often seek proof of his love and commitment. I was often consumed with doubt, and his reassurance was not always enough to allow me to just trust him. I guess this was more difficult because of the distance, and the relationship was still in the early stages. And sometimes my doubt arose because he said he would contact me at a certain time, but failed to. A little thing, but with all that distance between us I felt the doubt more strongly. Also, I've never had a serious relationship before, and my only experience was of being rejected in the early stages. I feared this happening again, even though I knew deep down that he was different.

On the night he arrived, I was again doubting him and fearing he was going to break up with me. I guess whenever I felt like this, part of me shut down as a way of protecting myself. He didn't break up with me and then it was just a matter of adjusting to being in each other's space again after four months apart.

Not long after his arrival, I began to be consumed with doubt again. This time I was convinced he was having a baby with another girl. I came to this conclusion by something that was said in an email from a friend of his, and also some other little pieces of 'evidence'. In my mind I could not think how it was anything other than true. I shut down. I couldn't connect with him. I talked to him, saying I had a nightmare about him having a baby with someone else. He reassured me that it was not possible. But no matter what he said, I think that was the beginning of the end for my feelings.

As I look back on the month he was here, I can see how the disconnection happened. I would get very upset by little things that he did, and shut off. I was not interested in affection past a certain point, and certainly not comfortable with anything sexual (we have never had intercourse by the way). I just didn't have the emotional connection to want those things. I then came to the heartbreaking conclusion that I didn't love him any more. I was filled with guilt and anxiety and panic. And of course he picked up on what was going on. He was very good about it, but I know he was very hurt.

I still have so much affection and care for him and I don't want to end things. But how do we carry on from here? I'm not happy living like this. And I know he is hurting. This man was going to be *the one* for me. We had talked about a future and I was so excited about it. Why don't I feel that any more? Can I get it back? I feel so betrayed by my own heart. Please help!

P.S. I'm 27 and he's 30.

Andrew writes:

I don't think you've been betrayed by your heart but by your head.

We imagine that the ability to think through a problem is always useful. How else will we find a solution? You're right, but like everything, it works best in moderation. There comes a point when we take random pieces of information—often from different parts of our partner's life— bolt them together and come up with a startling conclusion. For example, my boyfriend is not just having an affair but he's made his mistress pregnant! The more we think about it, the stronger the belief becomes and finally it crosses over from the product of our over-active imagination into a cast iron truth. I call this over-thinking.

After saying that you think too much about your relationship, I'm going to completely contradict myself because there are times when you don't examine your thoughts enough. I know this sounds weird but I'll explain. We imagine there is a straightforward relationship between an event and our feelings. For example, he doesn't return your call and you feel anxious. It seems simple but between action and feeling, there are lots of interpretations, assumptions and beliefs. For example, 'he doesn't love me as much as before' or 'if you love someone you check your phone every few minutes in case your beloved has texted' and 'even if you're at work, you should still return a message from your beloved within half an hour'. If these are your beliefs, you will feel rejected or doubt his love. However, there are a million other possibilities for not returning your call. He has run out of battery. His best friend picked up his phone thinking it was his and walked off with it. He's in the middle of a three hour movie and switched off his phone. His boss has given him two hours to write a five page report. I could go on with lots of neutral interpretations—all of which are less likely to make you anxious.

Moving on to beliefs, he could believe love isn't measured by how quickly he returns your text and therefore doesn't consider it a race against time. If you accept my idea that love moves through stages and the obsessive part does not last forever, you will accept slower responses or even forgetting to call to be natural (and possibly a good thing because if we spent all day texting we'd lose our job).

By now, you're probably going to be puzzled. How can I be both under and over-thinking and how do I find the right balance? Next time you find your brain going into overdrive, get out a piece of paper and start writing down all your thoughts. Next time you have an immediate and strong emotional reaction, again get out a piece of paper but this time ask yourself: what are my interpretations and my beliefs about this event? Once you've stopped and examined your reaction, write down your findings.

In the first part of this exercise, don't edit your thoughts or question your beliefs just get everything down on paper. In part two, you go item by item down your list and test each one. What is the evidence for this thought? Would it stand up in a court of law? What is the evidence to the contrary? If something seems preposterous once it's out of your head and on paper, cross it out. Next, look for exaggerations, 'he's ALWAYS forgetting to call when he said he would'. Always? Is twice in the last six weeks really always? In this case, you would change it to something more nuanced like 'he sometimes forgets to call'. Still upsetting but it's become more a thing guys do than revealing the truth about his deepest and darkest feelings. Other words to look out for are *should* and *must* (says who? your mother, your best friend, the Pope, all right thinking people?), *never* (which is the opposite of always and therefore too absolute) and *nobody* (I bet there's someone who, for example, cares or loves you).

Focusing on your beliefs, could they have been true when you were a child (and had fewer options) but are they out of date now you're an adult? Is this your mother or father talking but you've swallowed their beliefs whole? What do *you* believe?

Once you've tested all the interpretations, thoughts and beliefs, you'll probably find there are still one or two issues left. Hopefully, you will be feeling relatively calm and no longer overwhelmed. Finally, you can discuss these issues with your boyfriend and find out what he thinks rather than second guessing him.

What is love? *Something that is not just black and white.*

28. I don't know how to get rid of the feeling that something is lost in the relationship between me and my live-in boyfriend. He's English, I'm French and we're now moving to France for a year so I can be with family and he can practice his French. There's been a lot of tension about this, he's obviously nervous about moving countries.

Currently, I'm in France and when he joins me it will have been six weeks since we last saw each other. It's never been that long before. I do miss him and I think of him, I just don't have that feeling. I want it back and I feel that maybe it is my fault.

He's told me that I'm not communicating and that he doesn't know what I feel. I've had issues in the past with friends and loved ones letting me down; I try to talk, but I don't know what to say— I just get very upset and then get embarrassed about being upset. We are close and can discuss things, but I'm afraid that he will think that I'm needy and clingy, so I rarely ask for help, something that seems to frustrate him.

Two weeks before I left for Paris, we broke up but made up later that night. He said he didn't feel that I relied on him and told him things. Ever since I've felt a bit empty and heartbroken, even though we've continued kind of like before. I love him but sometimes I just feel nothing. I'm afraid of talking with him about it in case it just starts the argument all over again. I feel like I'm ruining it all despite really trying hard to show that I care.

Andrew writes:

I wonder if it's not so much that you've lost that feeling for your boyfriend but that you're frightened. By agreeing to move to France with you, he has revealed just how much he loves and cares for you. On one hand, that's great. But on the other, it means that your relationship is really serious—not just live-in boyfriend but maybe together forever. As you admit, you're frightened of being let down and although you can trust him enough with your heart to be boyfriend and girlfriend, this is a whole new level.

I also think you've fallen into a trap that I see over and over again. In order to feel secure, you like lots of closeness and intimacy. No wonder six weeks apart has made you anxious. However, our society puts great store on being independent and self-sufficient and can categorise what makes you feel happy and secure—like regular text messages and doing lots of things together—as 'needy and clingy'.

So let me say something that can't be repeated too often—everybody has different needs, wants and beliefs about relationships. Some couples spend most of their free time together while others rate separate interests as vital for the success of their relationship. There is no right or wrong answer, it's what works for each person and each couple. So please reframe 'needy and clingy' as 'I like to feel really connected to my partner'.

Fortunately, you have a boyfriend who seems comfortable with intimacy and, in fact, is asking you to be open and honest about your feelings. Hurrah! So I think you need to take him up on his offer. You will probably find that he has concerns too. Once you both know the pressure points, you can discuss what can be done about them. For example, if you are worried about him knowing nobody in France and being completely reliant on you—so you don't get any time to yourself—you can build short time-outs into the weekend. Perhaps you could play tennis with friends on Saturday morning but spend the rest of the weekend together. Alternatively, if it is too much time apart that makes you anxious, you can discuss ways of managing absences and find a formula that helps you still feel connected.

Ultimately, once you start talking about something—even falling out of love—it will seem a little less scary and a whole lot more manageable. After all, you also have two heads rather than one sorting everything out.

What is love? *Showing your partner the real you.*

29. I love my boyfriend to my dying day, however I am terrified I have fallen out of love with him and the last thing on earth I want to do is hurt him.

We met three and a half years ago. He is loving, kind, considerate, a wonderful man. It has been very stressful at times; I went through a lengthy court case with him and stuck by him. It upsets me to the core to see him suffer. Sometimes I look at him and he has the world's troubles on his shoulders. He is a good man, a gentleman and a gentle man.

Our relationship was happy, we communicated well, trusted each other, and we grew together... although our sex life had waned over the last year. We do share and have our individual own friends. My boyfriend is in a band as a hobby, I'm not so great at having outside interests. At times we had our ups and our downs (like small money worries, low confidence days etc.) but he was my love, my best friend, my lover all rolled into one.

Due I think to the stresses, I did have the odd fleeting doubt over the years which passed quickly. However, over the last six months, I had begun thinking about my ex a lot. He was my first love before my boyfriend, it was a very unhappy and unhealthy relationship, which I ended seven years ago. A few months ago, I started to dream about him—almost on a daily basis. I'd wake thinking I was back with him and I was happy in my dream. I ignored it when I woke up, but it always crept back. Then three weeks ago, I had a chance meeting with his friend. I was very upset and shaking, this friend had phoned my ex to say he was talking to me and my ex asked for my number... and I gave my number.

I was shocked at myself, felt sick and guilty all the time. I was a mess. I wanted my ex to call me then I didn't. One minute I wanted to get back with my ex then the next I didn't want to see him. I could not hide this from my boyfriend and I could not lie to him so I told him everything.

I feel all this and especially my reaction resulting from this chance encounter has shaken my relationship to its foundations. How could I react like this if I am supposed to love my boyfriend, the man I thought I was ready to spend my life with? I thought about a future with him and I felt numb. How could I feel numb about someone if they are the love of my life?

As the weeks have passed since that chance meeting, I have been going through turmoil, guilt, numbness and confusion. I finally realised my ex is not the one for me, for the first time I feel ready to let him go. However, I have been devastated over what this whole situation means for me and my boyfriend. We were looking to buy a house before this happened. Now our world is upside down.

My boyfriend has been great through this, and even though he's hurting he's been giving me space. He said he doesn't want me to stay with him out of pity; I could never do that to him any-way. He said he can live without me but he doesn't want to. He says he will give me all the space I need and even if we don't make it through this we were worth it either way.

Is there anything that can be done to save our relationship? How do I know if we are right for each other? I'm so confused. I'm spilling my heart, but it has been good to write it down.

Andrew writes:

It sounds like you are often overwhelmed by the strength of your emotions. On one hand that's great because you feel the highs (when things are going well) but you're really pulled down by the lows (when there are obstacles). There's another problem. When the feelings are so intense, you think I MUST listen to them and therefore, for example, allowed your friend to pass on your number to your ex. However, feelings are just clues on how to react not instructions. As you've discovered, you need to think rationally too. After all, it would not be sensible to return to a relationship which was unhappy, unhealthy and broke your heart. In effect, we need HEAD and HEART to make a WISE decision.

As it so helped to write everything down in your letter to me, I think this might be the answer to finding a more balanced approach and smoothing out some of the wilder highs and lows. So please keep a 'feeling diary' and jot down every feeling (and the events or thoughts that triggered them). I've been back through your letter and pulled out some of the feelings: terrified, stressed, upset, sympathetic, happy, shaking, shocked, devastated, love, pity, confused, pain, doubt and good. Imagine that you're sitting by a river and watching all these emotions float past. You will notice something immediately, *no feeling lasts forever* (however good or bad) but is replaced by something else. I think you'll also find that there are more middling feelings than you imagine—like upset and good—but they tend to be forgotten and the strong ones remembered. However, they are just as valid and need to be witnessed too.

Slowly but surely, you'll discover that you don't need to immediately react to your feelings. You can stop and weigh up whether something is strong (but momentary and will pass and be replaced by something else so probably does not need attending to right now) or constantly re-occurring (and therefore is probably important and should be actioned). In this way, you can begin to *choose* how to react rather than being blown backwards and forwards by your feelings. You have also more time to *think* about important but less pressing issues. What is worrying you at the moment? What problem is not being discussed? What are you not getting round to doing? (For example, finding your own outside interest to match your boyfriend's band.) In this way, your feelings have prompted some intensive questioning and thinking and will generate a wise plan of action.

When you're keeping your feeling diary, I think you'll also be surprised how often love comes floating down the river. Of course, you'll also find annoyance, irritation and anger at times—but that's only natural when two people live together, so don't let it knock you off course. Instead, learn the lesson and see what comes next—most probably the relief of making up and a little joy for finding a way through a problem together.

What is love? *One of the many feelings that we have every day, all of which need to be witnessed and taken seriously but not necessarily acted on immediately.*

30. I've been married 17 years, with my husband for 19 years, and have three wonderful children, 12, 11 and 9. I am the one that feels 'not in love' but, as you explain in your book, it was a long time before I disclosed it. I became the nagging wife, until I knew we had to talk seriously—even then those conversations didn't go so well.

Then I came across someone I knew as a teenager on Facebook (so cliché, I know) which prompted me to sit down with my husband and tell him I didn't feel in love with him. He didn't take me seriously and assumed once I had got things off my chest and stopped 'complaining' that I was happy. We didn't adequately address the problems and then a few years later I had another affair (this time for real). He discovered it but instead of denying it, I told him I was guilty and instead of begging for forgiveness, I told him I wanted out. I felt like I got divorced in my head years ago when nothing changed. I told him I would have done the honourable thing and divorced first but I wanted the kids to grow up in a house with both of us.

After a couple of months of cooling off, and entering therapy six months ago (three counsellors, his, mine and ours), I am not really seeing any significant changes in what brought me here in the first place except that he says he wants to change.

He is just not a very expressive person and I can't feel the love he offers because it doesn't work for me. He can't understand why I need what I need and finds it hard to give me something he doesn't understand himself. I find the conversation boring, there is no fun or spontaneity in our marriage, going out with friends feels like babysitting to me and I know there is no passion or romance. I still long for how I felt during my affair (even though I understand that is only a temporary feeling) as with that person the communication was just more natural and heartfelt.

I guess my question is, how long is reasonable to voice your concerns, try to address them and not get anywhere before you feel you did everything you could? The sad thing for me is that I recognise what is missing, have tried to address it calmly and even not so calmly but just feel like I am spinning my wheels.

I have three amazing children and I want very much to keep us together but I want equally as much to be happy and feel connected, and not just at rare moments.

Andrew writes:

Thank you for your interesting question. It is hard when someone says 'I love you' and 'I want to change' but you don't feel any evidence of the first and or see enough evidence of the second. So I can understand your frustration, however I wonder if you're asking the wrong question. Instead of asking, how long do I keep trying, I think you should be asking yourself a whole host of different questions.

Firstly, what's stopping me from feeling connected to my husband? My guess is that you're still in mourning for your affair partner. It is only natural to think about him and wonder 'what if'—that's part of the natural grieving process—and, not as some people think, evidence that you should be together. So give yourself time, the affair will recede into the background and you'll maybe feel connected with your husband for more than 'rare' moments. I also wonder if you're angry with him but can't express it because you're the 'guilty' partner and he's been so 'forgiving'.

Secondly, am I expecting too much for any relationship? In popular songs, all we need is the 'power of love' because 'you lift me up' or 'love conquers everything' and 'you light up my life' etc. The myth of love is that it will save us—and maybe you do need 'saving'. However, rather than looking for the 'connection of love' to make you feel better, I think you need to look deeper. Why does your life seem empty and meaningless? Do the children need you less and you're wondering what to do next with your life? Do you have low self-esteem or a painful childhood and hope love will make things better? Could you be asking love to fill a hole inside?

Thirdly, am I expecting something from my husband that's beyond his pay scale? By this I mean are you expecting your husband to make you feel better about yourself. Of course our partner is there to help us over the obstacles but they can't carry us through life. Ultimately, we have to take responsibility for our own stuff.

Finally, have I really tried everything? For example, have you asked for what you need in a way your husband can understand. By this I mean instead of asking for more 'fun' which is too general for most men, you ask for something specific—like to take jive dance classes together. You could also look at the different ways that you both communicate love (because your husband must truly be in love to hang in through nagging, an almost affair, a real affair and buckets of criticism!). In effect there are five love languages: Creating quality time together (dates, shared hobbies and even just lying on the sofa watching TV together); caring acts (running a hot bath for you, picking you up from the airport at 3am, gluing back together your grandmother's broken vase); appreciative words (I love you, compliments, talking about deepest secrets); affectionate physical contact (cuddles, kisses and of course sex); and present giving (thoughtful birthday presents and spontaneous little gifts like flowers or a bar of chocolate).

Unfortunately, we expect our partner to speak our language and don't recognise when he or she is showering us with love in his or hers. I would also consider taking away the 'ticking clock' (change or I'm out the door)—because under these circumstances he is probably anxious and stressed as he's expecting you to hold up a score card. If I'm being really honest, I'd also consider finding a different couple therapist—especially if your sessions have become a litany of what's wrong with your relationship because he or she is just listening and allowing you to get everything off your chest (but making you both feel helpless and the situation hopeless). You need someone who will roll up his or her sleeves, teach you better communication skills and find different ways of being together.

Having asked you so many questions, I will try and answer yours. This is not a quick fix. It will take time to consider everything on my list and work through your own half of this marital problem—rather than just getting divorced in your own head and hoping for the best or expecting your husband to do all the changing. Therefore, I would suggest giving it at least another year to 18 months and then having another review.

I know this sounds hard work (and you're tired and demoralised) but you've already learnt a lot about relationships and work on yourself is never wasted.

What is love? *Learning to appreciate how your partner communicates his or her love rather than demanding it in one particular way.*

TORN IN TWO

31. I have been meaning to write to you for quite some time about the 'greatest' personal conflict I have faced in my life. I have been married to my wife for nearly 10 years and we have two adorable children together.

I have recently started an affair (began two years ago) with my ex-girlfriend (who was my first love). I confessed about my infidelity and naturally my wife was devastated. However, I couldn't tell the full extent of my affair to her at once—or that it was still continuing—as I feared she would react very violently (and rightly so!). However, within months after I first told her, she found out and questioned me about it all and I told her everything. I was completely (mentally, emotionally and physically) attached to my girlfriend by then. Despite all the bitterness, anger and sadness my wife has been good to me throughout the last year and has always wanted to try to save our marriage.

I've been very unsure whether I can give anything back to my wife in return. Over the years I feel our relationship has become like two friends taking care of two little children. There is barely any physical desire in me for her (from much before my affair). I genuinely care for my wife's well-being and I love my children to the core, but I can't pretend to love her only to avoid hurting them. I have told her that I will not be able to continue our relationship as husband and wife without any feelings between us. She gets very angry, very depressed hearing all this from me. But, she wants to try. I do not know what to do.

My affair happened because I loved my girlfriend very deeply since I was 17. And that love overcame the moral guilt that I felt when we started having the affair. It was very wrong, but it has happened. I really don't know what I should do at this point.

Andrew writes:

It is extremely painful being torn in two directions; not only are you hurting your wife but your girlfriend too. However, I was impressed that you decided to write to me rather than leap into the darkness. I've counselled lots of people in the same position and I can explain some of the pitfalls and how you can dig yourself out of this hole.

At this point, you imagine it will take a miracle to save the situation (whereas I'd say it needs lessons in communication, permission to ask for what you need and the skills to listen to each other). Guess what normally happens while you are passively waiting for a miracle? Someone else appears on the scene or you remember the special connection with an old flame (and forget the reasons why you split up). You start rewriting history and you tell yourself: 'My wife and I are wrong for each other.' You start looking for evidence and find plenty in all directions. Throw in the power of limerence and love seems the miracle solution to all your problems—except it will break your children's hearts and your wife will do anything (including look the other way while you romance your mistress) to save your marriage.

At the moment, returning to your wife and children does not sound very appealing, as all you can imagine is more of the life that got you into this hole in the first place. However, you could learn how to communicate properly and be assertive. One of the few positives that come out of affairs is that it normally helps couples focus on sex and improves things in the bedroom. So you *can* have a fulfilling relationship with your wife.

I bet at this point, you are thinking 'yes but...' because it sounds like a lot of work and quite frankly your heart isn't in it. So what would happen if you went off into the sunset with your girlfriend? I am afraid this picture is not pretty either. There is one positive in that you were lovers previously and so knew each other outside the affair bubble. However, you are likely to fall into the trap that I see over and over again with couples who started as an affair. As they have left their partners, this has to be FULL ON love.

It has to be perfect with bliss flowing like wine. In effect, the gods of love have destined that you should journey through life together. (That's because without these defences and justifications, the guilt of breaking up your marriage would be unbearable.) Unfortunately, there is no room in this picture for falling out or having arguments about day-to-day stuff (and we know that's not your forte any way). So guess what happens, you start burying stuff. Can you hear history repeating itself? However that's only a side order of problems, here comes the main meal.

Not only will your wife be angry, upset and uncooperative (because you didn't give her a proper chance to save the relationship) but your children will feel betrayed too. I know this is not about them but part of being a child is seeing everything through your own eyes. So they will see you as not only leaving their mother but leaving them too! Guess who they will take out all their frustration and unhappiness on? No, it's not you, because they love you. It will be your poor lover who will be the Wicked Witch of the North, the fairytale wicked step-mother and Voldermort rolled into one. Can you imagine how jolly weekend outings are going to be? The arguments between you and your girlfriend over what she sees as the kids' bad behaviour. Except, you'll feel guilty about the divorce so tend to side with them. I can't begin to tell you the misery.

So what would I suggest? You're not going to like my answer, but it is possibly the best in the long run. If you make a real attempt to save your marriage (and by that I don't mean keeping up secret Facebook interaction with your girlfriend) your wife will not only respect your attempts (and if it fails, be less angry and more accepting) but you could have everything you've ever wanted. A loving marriage, loving children and personal fulfilment.

If it doesn't work out, you'll have learnt important communication skills like speaking up when you have a problem rather than keeping everyone else happy. These will be an asset in any new relationship. Trust me, a sensitive and caring man like you will find—if the situation occurs—love somewhere down the line. Your children are much more likely to be accepting of a new partner if she was not responsible, in their eyes, for their mother's misery. Perhaps, most crucial of all, you'll be able to look yourself in the mirror again.

What is love? *Wonderful but not a magic solution to all your problems.*

32. My partner and I have been together for 28 years, married for 24, and have three children. I have not been happy with various aspects of our relationship for many years and have considered leaving on several occasions. We have not had an intimate relationship for about 10 years due initially to having a young child, but then we seemed to have different bedtimes and fell into a relationship of 'being friends'. Although I used to get angry and argue with him about many issues, I eventually felt I had to stop feeling so emotional about things as it was not achieving anything except making me feel worse. In the end I felt like I took on a parental role in the relationship (and still do feel this to some extent).

About five years ago, we went to Relate to find out where to go with things. My partner did not want the relationship to end and I did not want it to continue. Sexually it was dead for me and I no longer wanted to have an intimate relationship with him, he still wanted to and had felt that given time we could get intimacy back. My biggest concern was about the children and the effects of a separation/divorce on them.

Through the counselling, we came to an agreement whereby we would remain living together but have separate bedrooms and no intimacy and he had to accept that there was no chance of sex ever happening. We would try to have an amicable relationship and focus on working together for the benefit of the children. We acknowledged that one of the biggest risks to this set up would be if either one of us met someone else, we would face up to that issue if it ever happened.

This has worked reasonably well, but recently I have been feeling 'is this it?'. I got a new job and have tried to get new interests into my life, which have made me feel better about myself and a bit more settled. However a month ago I met someone else, and launched into a very passionate affair. This has taken me by surprise, both in that I would happily jump into bed with someone I barely know and with someone who is also married.

At first I just wanted this person and felt 'why not, it is just a bit of fun'. We were both in relationships that lacked sexual intimacy and therefore justified what we were doing on that basis. However, I really like this person, it is not just the sex and I have begun (rather late I suspect) to think of the consequences of my actions including the hurt it will cause to all.

My dilemma is what to do now? Obviously I need to end the relationship but that is going to be very hard and I am not sure I know how to do it. Also this situation has made me realise that I do want a relationship that includes sex and love, but that is not something I want or even think is achievable from my relationship with my husband.

Andrew writes:

It sounds like you have been on a huge journey recently and despite all the pain and heartache, I have this strange sense of joy. You don't want to live a half life any more. Hurrah! But I'm also aware that there will be a lot of pain on the road ahead for you, your husband, your lover and your children.

So where do you go from here? I think you're right that you do need to end this affair—not only because it is not going anywhere but if you do decide to end your marriage it will make everything more messy and harder for your husband and your children (who will be tempted to take sides). I think you also have to be honest with your husband about what's been going on. He will probably have guessed and your honesty now will open a variety of possible options.

You could find that he is incredibly jealous, it could be that he will confess to similar affairs and that you'll either reshape your old contract to stay together into an open marriage, seek help to reconnect sexually or agree to part amicably. Whatever happens, your honesty will allow you to remain friends and communicate better. In particular, I'd like you to change the dynamic where you've become his parent and he behaves like a child. Now it's easy to think, if he grew up I'd treat him as an equal but you're equally to blame for this unhelpful dynamic by behaving like his mother. Therefore, I'd like you to move into the more neutral adult mode because if you do, he will naturally move into adult too. So what constitutes being in adult mode?

1. *Keeping it in the here and now.* If you dredge up past problems, it will either come out as critical parent ('You're always burying your head in the sand') or whiny child ('You don't know what it's like to give up this relationship').

2. *Focusing on problem solving.* Ask lots of questions: how can we move forward? what are our options?

3. *Listening to your partner and asking for clarifications.* If you get defensive you can sound like a sulky child or go on the attack and become critical parent again.

4 *Not coming up with solutions for him.* I find this a lot—especially with people who go through everything in their head a million times over. Presenting someone with 'the answer'—rather than making them an equal partner in the process—makes you a nurturing parent and your partner into a people pleasing child or a rebellious teenager. Take time to explore the situation, understand both of your positions and only then move into action.

If you find this approach helpful, it's called Transactional Analysis. You'll find more about it in my books (see Further Reading) and in those of Eric Berne who is the founding father of this branch of therapy.

Finally, I would urge you not to panic or make any quick decisions. Read, think everything through, you've taken years to get into this mess, it will take time to get out of it but HONESTY is the key—with yourself and everybody else. There will be pain ahead but it's got to be better than where you are now.

What is love? *Something we hardly notice—like the air we breathe—until it disappears. At this point, love becomes so obsessive and so all consuming that it is painful.*

33. How shall I say this? I am the bad girl—I've had an affair. After watching your video about the 'Eight Types of Affair', I think mine began as a 'cry for help', and progressed to full out retaliation. In short, nearly every type of affair fits my description. I would not say I'm quite the Don Juan but I am beginning to think I'm heading that way. The problem is, I want the security of being married, but I find myself wanting to 'stay open' to possibilities. I'm happy with my life (in spite of severe hardships at times) but I am in no way satisfied.

I don't know whether to leave or stay. There are many reasons to stay (including the happiness of my children) but sometimes (every other day) the reasons to leave seem more clear—bearing in mind honesty and truth, which are of high value to me. I am not currently in a relationship outside my marriage, but I honestly wish I could be.

Feeling trapped.

Andrew writes:

It sounds like you're in a difficult spot. You are desperately unhappy in your marriage, so unhappy that you've had one affair and you're contemplating another. I wouldn't say it was a cry for help but standing on the top of a mountain and SCREAMING.

So let's start at the beginning, you don't sound like a bad girl to me but someone at the end of her tether. If you value honesty and truth, you will know that an affair will bring nothing but a bit of temporary relief (at the expense of blowing your marriage apart, horrifying your children and leaving you feeling terrible). However, staying in the status quo is not the answer either—because it sounds like you're about to crack and do something that will hurt everyone.

If you're thinking of leaving, please speak to your husband before it's too late. Time and again, I have men writing to me who are devastated. From out of the blue, from where they are standing, their wives tell them they are miserable and they want to leave. No matter how much they plead for a second chance, they are told it's too late. So tell him: 'I love you but I'm not in love with you' and see what he says. He might tell you: 'You know what... I feel the same way.' In which case, it's fairly straightforward and you can both go your separate ways. Alternatively, he might decide to fight for you and turn the relationship round.

When someone craves the security of marriage but wants to keep their options open, I nearly always find someone who's had a difficult childhood. (Perhaps their father left when they were young or their parents fought all the time.) On one hand, you want to be held and told—'everything will be fine'—but on the other hand, you are frightened to let people get close because you know how easy it is to get hurt.

So summing up, I don't think you need an affair but a therapist who will help you understand how you got to these crossroads and to challenge that negative voice inside your head that judges and ultimately convinces you: 'I'm a bad girl'. If you stop and step back, who does this voice sound like? Your mother? Your father? A step-parent? Next time it starts up make a conscious decision to think: 'Here you go again'. Just this simple step will distance you and make you realise that it is just an opinion of your behaviour and you don't have to adopt it wholesale.

What is love? *A gift that's harder to give to ourselves than to other people.*

34. I'm in my mid-thirties. I've been with my girlfriend for almost 14 years but unhappy for the last few. I have questioned if my feelings for her would be enough for the next step: marriage and children. I'm just not sure that she is the right partner. I felt she lost some of her energy and we live *beside* rather than *with* each other. Although she tried sometimes to get closer to me, I started to block the feelings. As you described in your book, I felt for her more like a friend but with no real passion.

I felt limerence for a colleague but after reading your book decided to stop seeing her. Soon after, I met another woman during a short vacation. We started emailing as she lives further away. I told my girlfriend about my doubts concerning our relationship; we lived another three months together without really talking through our problems (as she is not really open with her feelings and neither am I). In the meanwhile, I talked extensively to the other woman over the phone. Actually she talked much more about her feelings and so did I (which I always missed in the relationship with my girlfriend). After nothing had changed during three months (I also tried counselling for myself), I left my girlfriend and moved out of our apartment. I told her that I need to have space for myself and sort my feelings out.

I started seeing the other woman and we met every second weekend. I told her from the beginning that I still had feelings for my ex but we decided we would try nevertheless and see how it goes. During this time, I met my ex a few times and we really talked for the first time. I thought it might have been a mistake leaving her without giving our relationship a real chance.

It's been another four months and I am totally confused because I can't get a clear picture about my feelings: I think my ex still loves me (although I also told her about the other woman)—one day I think it could work and the next I still have my doubts. I see her twice a week and we talk about what we expect from a relationship but I am really unsure how my feelings should look to start a second attempt. Am I just feeling guilt for myself and pity for her or can I build up feelings as you describe them in your book as a basis for a successful, long lasting partnership?

Maybe the problem lies more with me (I now started counselling sessions again). I am so afraid to get back to the situation I was in last year and potentially hurt her again if my feelings do not get any stronger. At the same time, I also miss the other woman because I built up a deep connection with her (I think because she is different from my ex). Somehow I am stuck in the middle and do not see any promising way out.

Andrew writes:

First off, I was impressed by the amount of thought you've put into thinking about your dilemma. You're right! The problem probably lies with you, so I'm glad that you've started counselling again. Rather than talking about your feelings—and trying to decide which woman to plump for—I would discuss 'endings' with your counsellor. How did your family deal with death and bereavement? Was it something discussed or hidden away? Why do you find it so hard to make a proper ending, mourn and finally heal and move on? Sometimes, the problem is not just that we don't know how to handle endings but that we tend to confuse craving and mourning. It is part of the grieving process to think about an ex, what went wrong and to ask 'what if'. Unfortunately, we mistake that for craving for our ex, imagine we should be together and phone them up (feeding the ache so that before you know it you are more confused than ever before).

So what about these two women? Affairs—and this is how the second relationship started even if it was only an inappropriate friendship at the beginning—are constructed in a bubble (and protected from the real world by secrets and fantasy). Not surprisingly, this is no foundation for a real relationship. So I wonder if you love this other woman or your fantasy of how it could be with her. Next, we come to your girlfriend. I wonder why you haven't married her? After all, you've been together for 14 years. Relationships have a natural rhythm and I wonder if you are truly committed to her because too long on hold (without moving onto marriage or children) can eat away and destroy a perfectly good partnership. So another question to discuss with your counsellor: am I frightened of commitment?

It could be that individual counselling will prepare you for couple counselling and you and your girlfriend will be ready to argue, resolve your differences and fall in love again. It could be that you need time away from both relationships, to learn about yourself and finally to be ready to open your heart to someone new.

It sounds like you are at an important turning point in your life. Be brave, work hard at your counselling and don't be distracted by easy short-term solutions (like an affair) which actually set you further back.

What is love? *Something that can't be put on hold but needs to grow, mature and move onto the next stage.*

LOVE AGAINST THE ODDS

35. I wonder if it is really possible to save every marriage? Does this mean love can never die, even if you had a lot of conflicts and it feels like you don't know if you love each other. I only feel attraction very rarely; the last time was several weeks ago.

Andrew writes:

I think most marriages can be saved, especially if a couple has children and they want to sort out their problems. There are a few exceptions—abusive relationships (violence, addiction), unforgivable betrayal (gambling away the house, aborting your joint child/insisting on you aborting a child or an affair with someone like your sister), unsteady foundations (you got married within a few months of meeting), train track relationships (you've led separate lives for a long time and neither partner is prepared or has the energy to change) or mid-life revolution (one partner wakes up one day wanting a totally different life and despite all the pleas from their partner to work on the relationship refuses to listen).

However, it is certainly possible that love can die—especially if it's not fed with kind words, loving actions, quality time together, physical affection or thoughtful presents. If you're seldom feeling any attraction to your partner, it is probably down to anger, resentment or sadness—all things that block out love.

My guess is that you're unhappy, in pain and trying to explain everything to your partner but he just criticises or walks away. Normally people become defensive like this because they are overwhelmed or feel criticised themselves. If you get very emotional when you talk—this can be overwhelming for men. We are trained to 'sort out problems' and a torrent of unhappiness is simply impossible to digest and therefore we switch off. So think about this calmly... what one small change could your partner make to help you feel better. Once you've decided on this, simply tell him. 'I love you but it would really help me to feel sexy if you gave me more complements.' Try not to ask for something negative... like 'stop flirting with other women' as this will make him feel criticised. Instead, frame it as a positive: 'I love it when you make me feel like the only women in the world as that turns me on.'

For most changes to stick, there has to be something in it for the other person. So ask your partner what *you* could do differently. You might get a torrent of suggestions but take a couple of deep breaths. Witness the upset and name it to yourself, for example, 'I'm feeling anxious' or 'I'm feeling misunderstood'. You'll be surprised to learn that this not only diminishes the pain slightly but also promotes a clear enough head to respond with an open heart (rather than striking back, defending yourself or closing down). When you're a little calmer, ask him: 'what change, in particular, would you like?'

Hopefully, you will find two changes of matching size. Keep an eye on how he does with his new behaviour and reinforce it with compliments and thanks. Slowly but surely, you'll discover that overcoming obstacles together can be more bonding than all the presents, romantic nights out and good things of life.

What is love? *Something that can be made stronger by adversity.*

36. Having had your book *How Can I Ever Trust You Again* fall out of my husband's car glove box onto my knee, whilst putting his satnav away, I am hurt, upset and ache so much inside. After having the ILYB conversation a year ago my husband had a mental breakdown, for which he still takes antidepressants, but I am finding the situation increasingly difficult to cope with.

I would have left long ago, but having four children am compelled to keep family life together for them and the fear that my husband will make things extremely difficult for us all if we were to separate/divorce. (When I applied for divorce after the ILYB he turned the elder two against me so I withdrew the application.) He does love me and insists on doing shopping, housework etc. and he has been the best father to our children but I feel completely numb and just want a proper man who will look after and care for me.

Furthermore, the children and family members have seen instances that could be regarded as 'mental abuse'. I have never been allowed to go out with friends or do my own things when he and the children are at home—some changes have been made and I go on occasional evenings out and odd fitness classes. However, too much has happened and I really do not want to continue the rest of my life like this... but what do I do?

Andrew writes:

I hope your letter will be an important lesson for men whose wife has said 'I don't love you any more.' Their goal might be to get their wife back but at what cost! You have lost all respect for your husband, your problems have gone from bad to worse and at this rate you *will leave*—not tomorrow or the day after but some day—unless there are some major changes.

To be honest, I wish it was your husband writing to me because he has turned a difficult situation into an almost impossible one. At the risk of getting you to communicate through my books, I would be tempted to suggest leaving another book, *My Wife Doesn't Love Me Any More*, in the glove compartment for him to find! As it would explain what he's doing wrong and provide some of the skills necessary to dig himself out of this dark hole.

However, it's not him that's written but you. I hope you understand that you *truly* have my utmost sympathy—to feel trapped and manipulated is horrible—but you need to understand your role in this. One line in your letter particularly struck me: 'I want a proper man who will look after and care for me'. How old does that make you sound? To me, it sounds like a little girl who wants a daddy to kiss and make it better. I hate to be brutal but we need to look after and care for ourselves (our partner should be someone to journey through life with, who will pick us up when we fall, but not carry us). I say this for two reasons—and sorry if I've upset you—but you've taken this role for your husband. You've been his 'all caring' mummy. He throws a tantrum (about you leaving him) and you've come running back. It gets exhausting parenting our partner, so I'm not surprised you want a bit of parenting yourself. But you're setting up your husband for a task that he will never be able to achieve (and making yourself angrier and more trapped too).

So what can you do? You need to approach him adult to adult. (This is Transactional Analysis or TA for short, see Further Reading.) Don't bury your needs—to keep the peace—as they will burst out angry, domineering and scare the living daylights out of him (so he becomes a pathetic heap of jelly that just makes you angrier). Be calm, report your feelings: 'I feel... when you... after... because...' rather than acting them out with sighs, pointed comments and rolling eyes. Deal with one issue at a time. 'I am thinking of going out on x day...' in an assertive manner. Remember my slogan, he can ask (for example, don't go out tonight), you can say no (or maybe) and the two of you can negotiate (and either find a compromise or do a trade where you'll do x for him if he does y for you).

Finally, when he does things that are close to mental abuse, don't push it under the carpet but explain why it's not acceptable. The same with involving the children in your stuff. Don't threaten but explain how he is pushing you further away. My hope is that if treated like an adult, he will start to behave like one. Who knows the situation might improve, you might even start to like him again!

What is love? *An equal partnership.*

37. Can you help me? I'm at my wit's end. I have been with my husband 28 years altogether and married for 20 of those years. All in all, we have what I thought was a good marriage though we don't argue. About 11 weeks ago, I discovered he was having what you would call an inappropriate relationship with a married woman who has a young family, about 10 years younger than him. He says its been going on for about a year. We have talked through anger and then tears. He says there is no sexual relations between them which I do actually believe but he's texting and meeting her. Initially, he was going to leave and said she was going to leave her husband also. However, 11 weeks on, he is still here in the house, still seeing her and she is still with her husband.

I have read *How Can I Ever Trust You Again* twice over, and it has been a great help to me in my darkest hours. I have told him that he should go until he decides who he wants but he obviously doesn't want to. No one, apart from one of his close friends, knows he is having this affair which is I think another reason for him not wanting to go. I have spoken to my friends and used them as unpaid therapists! He says he still loves me but has lost the 'feeling' that he once had and that he really doesn't know what he wants. I have tried to act normal and put this to the back of my mind.

However, today, I passed this woman on the way in to hospital when I was visiting my elderly mother. It is the first time I've seen her and I've been in bits since. I feel unattractive and old as she looked much younger. It has just brought it all back to me and I realise that he shouldn't be treating me like this and that I am allowing him to do so. The problem is I love him and I really don't want him to go. After reading most of the emails people send to you, I realise that most affairs generally finish once the other partner finds out or at least they pretend to finish it whereas he's not. I'm not quite sure what this relationship actually is but I'm afraid if I let it continue any longer, as you say, it will develop into something more serious and I feel I'm running out of time.

Andrew writes:

My alarm bells rang the moment you wrote—'we don't argue'. Frequently, couples fall out of love not because they argue too much—but because they don't argue enough. All the inevitable issues that come from two people living together, changing and growing get buried under a comfortable easiness and one day someone wakes up and discovers the only reason they've managed to stay is because they have switched off their feelings.

Unfortunately, ILYB often turns into an affair if it is not dealt with soon enough. Fortunately, all the anger comes up to the surface in the aftermath of discovery. What worries me is that you and your husband have settled back into denial. He's pretending its OK to pour all this emotional energy into this other relationship and leave you with the scraps. NO WONDER HE DOESN'T FEEL ANYTHING FOR YOU. You can see that I'm getting angry, a sure sign that you should be feeling angry too rather than sinking into depression and self-criticism.

Before seeing the other woman, you were in denial. You were hoping if you kept your head down, somehow he'd wake up and realise his mistake. But please use this chance meeting as a wake-up call!

What should you do? This is the tough bit—but I can promise you that doing nothing is the least promising option. Okay. Affairs thrive on secrecy, so I think you should give him a choice. Give up the other woman and work on your marriage or leave and go to the other woman. It is simply not acceptable that she can enter your house at any moment through texts and emails. If he continues to sit on the fence, I would tell him that you can no longer remain silent (and protect him) so that means telling his mother, sister and other family members.

None of the options are very appealing, but I think you need to get back in touch with your inner anger again. Anger gives you energy to get things done and makes you stand up for yourself.

What is love? *Opening your eyes to what's really going on.*

38.

My partner and I are engaged and have been for nearly a year—we have just had a gorgeous baby boy that we love more than words can say.

Things have always been quite rocky. My partner hasn't helped with our son at all—he is now eight weeks old—but was apparently 'working' when he was at home. He would expect me to cook and clean, telling me that my first priority is our son while his first priority was work.

Today he sent me a message saying that he spoke to my cousin about things and when I asked what things, he said he felt as if he is suffering from depression. I rang him straight away and asked why he couldn't talk to me about it and he said because I don't support him in anything he does—which is a complete lie.

He is the only one working but instead of saving to buy a house or saving to pay for our wedding next year he spends money on new sporting equipment and memorabilia. He spent $5000 the other week which could've bought us something that we need as a family.

He says he has all these plans for us but it seems that he doesn't want us to get there any time soon. I don't think he understands the difference between 'wants' and 'needs'.

Andrew writes:

If I had to name one problem that causes more relationship unhappiness than any other, I'd probably plump for 'needing to always be right'. Of course, it's perfectly understandable because we're told from an early age—sometimes explicitly but more often covertly—'if you're good then good things will happen'. Obviously, there is a flip side: 'Bad things happen to bad people.' No wonder we will defend our actions to the hilt. We need to be the good guy to feel safe. Therefore we have to paint our partner as the baddie. This process of making ourselves whiter than white might be perfectly understandable but always being right dramatically decreases the odds of love thriving.

Let's look at your letter. Your partner is depressed, pours out his heart to his cousin and tells them he doesn't feel supported. Instead of trying on this idea and seeing how he's come to that conclusion, you dismiss it outright. In fact, it's not just a lie but a COMPLETE lie. OK, you can tell yourself you're still the good guy because you've done all these great things to support your partner. (Maybe you've even come up with a list.) Meanwhile, your partner is the bad guy because he doesn't appreciate all you've done for him and he's a liar too! Not only does this make you angry—and drives a wedge between the two of you—but he's unlikely to tell you his problems again because he doubts he'll get a fair hearing and probably a load of criticism too.

It's the same with money. You believe that anything spare should be spent on your wedding and family needs. Once again, you're right because, in your opinion, you're considering everybody's needs. Meanwhile, he's wrong because he's being selfish and getting sports equipment that only *he* wants. However, let's step back and look at weddings. While most little girls dream of their wedding day and as adults turn choosing cake, dress and party favours into a hobby, I've yet to meet a heterosexual man who gave a second thought to his wedding day (before his fiancée sat down with a list). Many grooms would be perfectly happy getting married in clothes they already own and going down the pub with their mates afterwards. What really drives up the cost of weddings is what the bride wants. So sure, say the wedding is for both of you but be honest enough to admit it's *your* wants that are driving up the bills.

Guess what happens in your partner's head? You've got it. He thinks he's in the right too. He *needs* the sporting equipment to help cope with the stress of work (which has just multiplied tenfold because he's the only bread winner). You're in the wrong because you've got so upset about a measly $5000. I could go on but you've hopefully you've got the picture. He's painting you as the bad guy too!

At this point, I bet you're feeling really low, defensive and probably saying 'yes but...'. Please forgive me, I don't want to make you feel criticised. I'm sure you got enough of that as a child. (In fact, most people who tend to throw around blame need to feel 'right' because they had tons of blame poured over their heads as kids, were made to feel unlovable if they were 'bad' or only acceptable if they were perfect little girls or boys.) That's why, I want to introduce you to a simple idea that will turn round your relationship: *Everything is six of one and half a dozen of the other.* You're both equally responsible for everything that's good and everything that's bad in your relationship. That's right, the good *and* the bad.

Let's look at the particulars of your situation, your lives have undergone a huge change. You've moved from being a couple to a family. You've given up work. He's got to provide for three (not just half of the monthly budget as before). Having a child is a big adjustment and you need time for everything to sink in. It's terrifying having all that responsibility and babies bring up lots of stuff from our own childhood (for example, being blamed or not feeling good enough). So I'd like to say you're *both* right to feel stressed but what counts is how you're going to resolve these problems. In my book that involves talking, listening without judging and finding a solution that works for both of you.

What is love? *Giving up your need to always be right.*

39. After 31 years and out of the blue I get the ILYB... I am totally devastated! And yes there is an emotional affair going on. We are at 'crisis point' and living separately. Your book *I Love You But I'm Not in Love With You* is great, just what I needed to read right now, but there doesn't seem to be any counsellors that deal with trying to rebuild a relationship in my area. They all are happy to take my money and tell me I am broken hearted, but nothing to help me get my husband back. How can I do this on my own?!

Andrew writes:

You're facing one of the biggest crises that life can throw at a woman but the good news is that there's lots you can do on your own to improve the situation. Here's 10 ideas to get you started:

1. Stop doing what doesn't work—for example, nagging, begging, manipulating. Basically what you know drives him up the wall—but when you're under pressure is the trap that you always fall into. Other traps include always wanting to talk about the relationship (which sucks all the life out of day-to-day living), trying to make your partner ashamed of his behaviour (which makes him feel so low, he has to reach for what makes him good—speaking to the other woman) or reaching for magical solutions (because you'll fall apart when they don't work, feel hopeless and helpless).

2. Write him a note telling him what you're going to do. The most important thing about my strategy is that it is up-front and open. So you tell him, 'I'm sorry that I have been... (insert your trap from part one). I've tested that to destruction and I know it doesn't work. If you catch me doing it again, please free to point it out.' (Obviously, you have to deliver on this promise.)

3. Don't be panicked by artificial ticking clocks. It took years to get into this mess. Don't expect to get out of it in seconds.

4. Think about your contribution to what went wrong and what you'd like to change.

5. When you've thought it through, set up a meeting with him. Apologise for your half of what went wrong and tell him about the sort of relationship you'd like in the future.

6. Listen to him—I call this active or deep listening. Don't defend. Don't justify or promise him it will be better. Just listen. Ask questions. Imagine everything he says is true (at least from where he stands).

7. Let things settle for a while after this conversation and think some more.

8. Suggest working on the relationship. Tell him, there are no pre-conditions. Working does not mean demanding it can be fixed. Explain, you won't be angry if you both try but your efforts fail. In fact, it will help the healing to have tried.

9. Don't be downcast by set-backs. It will take time but if you don't get angry and instead try to step into his shoes, he will come out of his bolt hole.

10. You might need help for part 8 (so that might be the time to see a counsellor).

Finally, I want you to be kind to yourself and forgive any slip-ups you make. I've helped hundreds of women in your situation and they all take two steps forward and one back. It goes with the territory. Find yourself a friend who will listen without advising and coming up with her own magical solutions or encourage you to give up every time you're down, and please arrange treats and nice things for yourself (because lots of women, when their husbands stop loving them, stop loving themselves too).

What is love? *Being able to give even when you're getting nothing back.*

MAKING AMENDS

40. I am stopping with my sister's family as home life had become a living hell. We have been together over six years (after meeting at work). She left her husband of seven years to be with me so it was not the easiest of starts. However, she said she did not know true love till she met me. We moved to our first flat together and were very happy when she became pregnant. It was love at first sight for me, and I still love her very much but I did not always show it after our son was born. His arrival completely changed the dynamics of our relationship.

After our son arrived her attention went mainly his way which is only natural, I know, and my attention went into my own world. It was a first child for both of us. She complains that I did not do enough to help when he was very young and she was finding it very tough, and I admit I could've done a hell of a lot more.

Nine months later our second son was stillborn prematurely at five months. This really hit us hard as you can imagine and my way of dealing with it was to push it out of my mind. That was selfish of me and things have gone downhill from there.

I have repeatedly asked for a fresh start and promised I will do better but she says she does not believe me any more and needs space. She did tell my sister that she still loves me in some way but she is sick of me crying all the time, which I have been (because I am completely heartbroken and my world has been rocked by this). I don't understand why she won't give us another chance, if we both wanted it to be really good then it would be wouldn't it? I miss my family so much, it's tearing me up living like this.

Since I left she is now trying to arrange a mortgage on her own. The only options I can see for my next step are:

1. Go back home, which I don't think will go down well after she said she needs space.

2. Stay at my sister's for a while which is a little bit awkward and it looks like I'm doing nothing.

3. Rent a flat and get on with my life while hoping that absence makes her heart grow fonder and she thinks again.

Maybe getting my own place could be the final nail in the coffin. I am a laid back person who still works in a factory that I said I would not be in for very long when we got together; she is a very ambitious Polish girl who I met there and she is now heading for a manager's job in a recruitment agency. I am desperate to get back what we once had but while I look back at the amazing love we shared she looks back at all the disappointments I caused her. I realise on paper it doesn't look good and it isn't but I just need to know if I have even a tiny chance of winning my family back and righting a wrong or should I just let go of the pain of the past and restart my life on my own.

I did ask her to read your book but she said she does not need a book to tell her how to feel. She put a post on Facebook intended for me stating the way to get started is to quit talking and start doing. But do what?

Andrew writes:

Of course, there is a tiny glimmer of hope. In fact, it's quite a big one. She is telling you what she wants: action not words. If she wasn't interested, she would have shut down completely.

So how do you fight back? Firstly, stop emotionally dumping on her and trying to guilt her back into your life. It's just pushing her away. The same goes for pleading, begging and promising to change. Whenever you're tempted to slip back into your old behaviour remember this mantra: if you're in a hole, stop digging. What I'd like you to do is *prove* you can change. So where do you start?

I'd like you to make a list of everything that you regret from the past. From your letter, I would put 'not supporting her' with your son and over the miscarriage. (I can't tell you how many times I've counselled men who have tried to be strong or thought sharing their sorrow would make their wife's grief worse but just ended up making her feel alone or worse still that he didn't care about losing the child.) I'm sure you can come up with many more regrets. Write them down because that will make them more real and provide a constant reminder of what needs changing.

Next, brainstorm with your sister everything you could do which would demonstrate that you mean business. I would start with your job. If it's dead end, start applying for others. Take some courses to improve your qualifications. Offer to take more responsibility at your current job, so your prospects will improve there too.

If renting a flat is least worse of the options, that's what you'll have to do. OK it doesn't make sense to you but you've got to start putting yourself into her shoes. She wants you to take control rather than expect her to sort this out. I'd also like you to consider how you come across to your wife. I know this is going to sound harsh but I think it's best to be honest. You sound like a puppy dog, begging for attention. That's not only very unsexy but really tiresome too. I bet she would like you to be an equal partner.

At this point, you're ready to make a Fulsome Apology. This is not just saying 'I'm sorry' over and over again or beating yourself up to prove how bad you feel about your behaviour. It has three elements:

1. Acknowledges what you've done wrong. (Your list will come in handy.)

2. Accepts responsibility. (Rather than offering explanations as these come across as excuses.)

3. Explain why it's not going to happen again. (Go through your plan of action and tell her what progress you've made with each item—however small.)

Please don't expect her to fall into your arms or say everything is forgiven. She might even be dismissive or plain cold. However, it will register and over the next few days she will probably soften—as long as you keep focused on making changes and driving forward toward your new goals.

Sadly, there is no magic solution—it will take time. However, I do think that you're determined to win her back. So work on yourself and being the man that she would like to be with—rather than expecting her to take you back (and then become that person).

What is love? *More than just a feeling but something that is followed up by loving actions.*

41. I am 40, my wife is 35 and we have two children, 6 and 9. We have been married for 10 years. A few months ago, my wife dropped ILYB on me completely out of the blue. I was devastated. I had no idea she was having these feelings. We spoke, very emotionally, about the situation, and she revealed that she had begun to feel differently about two years before.

I met my wife at our place of work when she was 17, but we didn't start our relationship until she was 21. During those years we both had other partners and were just friends, although it's no secret that I fell for her the day we met. My wife never had a large circle of friends other than those at work and as a result never had much of a social life outside our joint friends. This changed when our youngest started school and my wife made some very good friends with other mums from school, and she also joined the PTA. This was great news, as I had my own activities on certain days, and I had begun to feel that she was tied to the house and could resent me for going out.

This brings us to two years ago... A local social choir was created by one of the PTA members, for getting together, having fun singing and other social events. My wife jumped in with both feet; she now had another focus outside of being a wife and mum, and had her own identity. She became very popular within the group. During this time my wife also became very conscious of her appearance and spent a lot of time at the gym. She lost weight, changed the way she dressed, changed her hair, and started going out a lot more. I was genuinely happy for her.

Our sex life improved. Her socialising had led to her coming home after a few drinks, and she would wake me up for sex (which she had rarely done before). I was very happy, and I thought she was too. We were finally starting to enjoy each other again, like we had before the children.

Then without warning, ILYB. She explained that she had been struggling with her feelings for two years. She had contemplated different ways of getting the love back, but had found no solution, and the only option left was to split up. She spoke of divorce, selling the house and a host of other very final actions. Over the next few weeks it was tough. We shared the bed, but hardly spoke. I was off to work early, and the moment I stepped back in, she would be on her way out, not to return until after midnight. When we did speak it wasn't very fruitful. All she could say was, 'I don't know what I want, but I know I don't want you'.

I found it very hard to keep it together for the children. We are a very close family and there is no doubt they picked up on my sadness. I suggested counselling, but she said as there was no love for her, and she didn't want to be with me, there was no point. She was convinced she would be better off, and have a happier life with just the children. She wanted me to have all the access I needed, and didn't want to fight over them, and wanted to stay friends... Huh! How on earth was I going to be able to do that when she had ripped the heart right out of me. I packed a suitcase and told her I was leaving. She agreed a separation might be good for her.

A few weeks later she wanted to talk and said the time apart had given her space, relieved the pressure she had felt, and she now believed she wanted us to try to work it out. We saw a counsellor who was recommended by a friend, but by the end of the first session, the counsellor told us that we did not need joint counselling, that my wife possibly had personal issues to deal with and she was at a crossroads, so they should continue one-to-one.

On top of this, I recently lost my job, and have been effectively homeless (staying with various family and friends), jobless and with an estranged family. I have been at an all-time low. I am trying to pick up the pieces, but it has not been easy. Without a job I can't move on, and with low confidence I am finding it very hard to motivate myself to find a job. I am worried she will see me as a lost cause, and will find someone else. I am worried I am running out of time.

Andrew writes:

There is one idea that I want you to remember and hold onto. Most women with ILYB do not want to leave but their husband's anxiety can push them away. So if you can be calm and focused on improving your relationship and growing as an individual, you will come through this crisis with a better marriage.

So what's been going on for your wife? It is great to be childhood sweethearts and have been 'together forever'. However, as people approach 40, they look back at the paths they didn't take. What if I'd gone off to university? What if I'd followed my ambitions to be a rock star? What if I'd seen a bit more of the world before I settled down? This is a perfectly natural part of growing older and everybody goes through it—but it is more acute for childhood sweethearts who have had less opportunity to experiment. Around the mid-point in our lives, we become more aware of our mortality—perhaps one of our parents dies—and we start to calculate how much time we've got left and what we want to do with it. During this soul-searching, everything is up for debate and this includes our relationships—especially in two scenarios.

Firstly, your wife finds your marriage disappointing because she hasn't felt special or cherished. Secondly, the two of you have been so close and done so much together that it is hard to work out where, for her, being a wife and mother ends and being a person in her own right begins. She asks herself: 'Who am I?' 'What do I want from life?' As I hope you're beginning to realise, these are very difficult questions to answer and many people shy away from them. We want simple and easy solutions. So, many women go to the gym (to change the way they look) or go out more (to have a bit of fun). Alternatively, some women (and men too) are frightened of looking too deeply for fear of what they might find and the impact on the family: What if they do a lot of soul-searching and discover they are deeply unhappy, can't be themselves or that their husbands are stopping them from achieving their goals? Unfortunately, suppressing these thoughts doesn't make them go away but instead multiply until the wives confess: 'I don't love you any more' and 'you're holding me back.' For many husbands, this is a complete shock. They haven't prevented their wife doing anything. In fact, they have positively encouraged her to go out with her friends or been happy to babysit.

If your wife has become a stranger or seems to be going through a mid-life crisis, what should you do?

Embrace change

We don't like change. It is uncomfortable, scary and we do our best to avoid it. 'What if we grow apart?' 'What if she changes and wants different things?' 'What if she wants me to be the sort of man I can't be?' It is easy to catastrophise and imagine 'this is the end of our relationship!' However, while you are panicking, it is easy to overlook the upside. It would be a dull world if we were exactly the same at 17 and 47. It might feel comfortable to 'know someone inside out' or be able to predict the way they will react but it is also incredibly boring. What's more, 'possessing' someone kills passion, after all we desire what we haven't got—or at least don't feel 100 per cent sure of. (I bet that since your wife has threatened to leave, your interest in her has sky-rocketed!)

It is good, from time-to-time, to audit your life and put everything up for discussion. The problem is when some subjects are off-limits—like your relationship. As I've explained before, negative thoughts are better out than in—so they can be tested in the real world. Anything that is suppressed and 'unmentionable' grows power and becomes even scarier in the shadows.

So thank your wife for being honest and explain how her soul-searching has encouraged you to do something similar and tell her what you would like to change about yourself.

Be honest with yourself

Imagine everything your wife says is true—at least from her perspective—have you truly supported her changes? Have you agreed to babysit but only grudgingly, so your wife felt she could only ask occasionally? Although you haven't banned her from going out, have you used more subtle ways of getting your way—for example, sighing or sniping ('out again') or being passive aggressive (not leaving work on time, so you're back late and she misses the first part of her class)? Maybe you've appealed to her better judgement: 'We're happier just the two of us' or 'don't go because you'll never find anywhere to park'. Perhaps you've just assumed: 'We like a nice quiet weekend at home' or 'we don't like noisy clubs or pubs' and not checked out whether your wife agrees or not. If any of these strike a chord, make a fulsome apology (see page 108).

Become part of the change

If you genuinely believe that you have supported your wife, try going the extra mile. For example, helping set up the refreshments tent for her

PTA fund raiser or suggest inviting the members of her choir and their partners over for a barbecue. In this way, you will begin to know some of the personalities involved and, even better, when she needs help she can count on you. If she is taking a course, go along to the open day or read a set text so that you can intelligently discuss her interest.

Although it is harder to work on improving communication at a distance (it is the key to helping your wife fall back in love again), it is not impossible. There are lots of opportunities to listen, really listen to what she has to say, to be flexible (about picking up the kids) and be assertive about your needs too. I can understand how both losing your job and your wife can knock your confidence but sitting at home and despairing will only make you feel worse. Instead, each day set yourself some doable task for finding a new job—for example, phone three friends to tell them you're looking for work—by achieving these, you will gradually feel better about yourself. Good luck, keep believing and it will get better.

What is love? *Something that is always changing, growing and adapting as we mature and progress through the different life stages.*

42. I had finally found the only guy that has ever encouraged me to be who I am and love me as I am. He even moved to the other side of the world for me after I got a job overseas. The first year we were here together was really stressful for me, and I got depressed. He was my lifeline.

Then, just as I started to feel like I could get better, he gave me the ILYB line. We agreed to work on it. I did all kinds of research. I tried all kinds of things, and I asked him to do things with me. He kept saying, 'I'm trying but I don't think I can bring back those feelings I used to have.' And to me it didn't feel like he was trying at all because he kept doing things that really bother me... cancelling special plans at the last minute when someone else calls, not calling to say he is going to be later than expected, when I call to ask if he is okay or are his plans just running later than he thought, he says he's just leaving and then he doesn't even come back for anywhere from four to six hours. I finally had a talk with him that seemed really fruitful yesterday, like he was actually going to really start trying with me TOGETHER. Now, today he is telling me that while our coming weekend trip is a real shot for us to see if we can try to make the relationship work, he doesn't think we should live together after our lease is up.

Is it possible to live separately after having lived together and still fix the relationship? Because to me that just seems like the first step to ending and like he wants to make me feel better by saying that even though we aren't living together we can still be in a relationship. I am so devastated I can't even function, which doesn't help trying to fix it because I think it pushes him away. And I also live on the other side of the world where I don't have any family or friends but him. I am just so desperate; it's horrible. Is there any hope? My mom is sending me your book, and he agreed to read it, but whether or not he'll go through the exercises with me is a different question. I can't handle this. It's driving me deeper into depression than I was in the first place. Please help.

Andrew writes:

You partner is very important in your life and he sounds like a good guy who has helped you grow and become stronger. However, in your mind, you have turned him from a supporter into your life support system. He has been built up until he has almost god like qualities and holds your very survival in his hands. With this mindset, no wonder you are panicking. So take a deep breath and take a step back. You *can* handle and you *will* handle this.

Reading your letter, I am struck by all the things that you would like him to do for you. What about the things you could do for him? The truth about love is that it is a two-way street. You have to be his supporter too and change in ways that he will appreciate. One of the most important things that I have learnt from 30 years counselling couples is that for a change to stick, there must be some benefit for both sides. If he stops cancelling plans at the last minute, you will stop .... (fill in the blank). In this way, there is an incentive for both of you to keep the contract. It also makes the relationship more equal too. And when you have reached this point, your love for each other will not just survive but thrive.

I wonder if what's been going wrong with your attempts to resolve ILYB is that you've been focusing on things to bring you closer together again (and hopefully reawaken his feelings). However, if he's angry, sad, exhausted from so much giving (or whatever else), he will not want to make 'special plans' as this will seem like denying his feelings (and sweeping them under the carpet) or remind him of your overflowing heart and how empty he feels inside. Interestingly, when you had a long chat—and allowed him to pour out all his problems—the two of you felt closer.

I can't say this often enough, making amends is not just doing nice things together but facing the nasty things too (without panicking, shutting down or running away).

What is love? *Both partners supporting each other and helping each other grow.*

43. My husband gave me the ILYB speech nearly a year ago. We have been together since we were teenagers. I was devastated, with hindsight I can see our relationship was in the doldrums and that I had taken his love for granted. He agreed to go to counselling and over the months we have had many soul-searching conversations. I think we want very different things out of life. I am 48 and starting to think about slowing down and spending more time together, he is 49 and thinking about all the things he hasn't achieved. He also has ambitions about moving abroad which if I am honest I don't share, I'd find it difficult to leave my children, plus my mother who is unwell.

I have read your book and found it very useful in understanding our situation and helped to improve things between us. He tells me that he can't imagine life without me, however I feel that he is staying because it is convenient and I find this very hurtful. I feel I have let myself down by accepting this situation and on occasion my self-esteem is low. Our sex life has improved, but at times I feel I shouldn't be having sex with someone who doesn't love me.

My feeling are all confused, some days I am positive and think yes we are going to make it, on others I think it would be best to call it a day and try to rebuild separate lives and hopefully find happiness elsewhere. It's been nearly a year and I want to hear my husband tell me he loves me and if he can't tell me that then we shouldn't be together.

Andrew writes:

I'm glad that you found my book helpful. The counselling sounds positive. The sex has improved. Your relationship seems out of the doldrums but something is still not right. My suspicion is that you have not really talked about your different priorities for the future. At first sight, the fact that he wants to focus on new ambitions but you want to spend more time together seems scary. However, I am reminded of the times that I've had couples in therapy who have had startlingly different ambitions. We would duck round them and concentrate on the smaller issues, because the big ones seemed so comprehensively different and impossible to compromise.

I will let you into a secret, I was a bit of a coward. Often the couples were making progress and I did not want to jeopardise that. Yet time after time when we stopped avoiding the big issue and set aside a week (or even weeks) to talk about the controversial subject, the topic was covered in minutes rather than hours and a compromise readily found. It had become a paper tiger—by this, I mean something frightening on the outside but ultimately nothing on the inside.

So let's assume that your differing ambitions are a paper tiger too? Why not really listen to your husband's plans? Enter into them with an open heart and get all the details. Discover how they would work in practice—right down to the last detail. Make him feel that you have understood everything and entered into the spirit of his dreams; then tell him your remaining doubts. Go off on a few trips to research the possibilities together. (It will fulfil your desire to spend more quality time with him.) I'm sure that sort of gesture will make him open his heart to you in return. With that kind of understanding, it might be possible to find a way forward that will not mean deserting the kids or your mother but still provide him with fresh horizons and the two of you a new future together. Don't be afraid of a paper tiger.

What is love? *Staring into the darkness for long enough to discover some chinks of light.*

LOVE AFTER THE AFFAIR

44. I read your wonderful book *How Can I Ever Trust You Again* and it helped me a lot in my own relationship. I feel deep love for my boyfriend, even though our relationship is complicated. We met just over two years ago when I left my 20-year relationship for him. I split up with everything, my job, home, friends, to follow him to southern Europe (I am from the north).

I did understand that it might be hard for us. He is the kind of guy who always gets attention from women between 20 and 70 (he is 45); they are so attracted to him that all he has to do is snap his fingers. He is a very good dad to his children, five kids from three different mothers in three countries, and he always travels to be with them as much as possible.

He had affairs before we met, but I thought he would no longer feel the desire since I came into his life (how naive can I be?). Five weeks ago, I found out that he has been having an affair in Italy for months, as well as in Germany… three women (including me). It's not only sex, he found peace, freedom and understanding in the arms of these women, while we were always struggling and fighting.

He wants to forget the past, he has promised, but he is not willing to answer all my questions. He say that he loves me, that I'm the only one who counts… On the other side, I can't trust him, I don't know what he feels for the other women. I'm struggling.

Andrew writes:

The myths about love encourage us to think if we love each other enough everything else will be fine. So I'm not surprised that you have closed your eyes to the cold hard facts, i.e. he's a serial flirt with a history of infidelity, because your love will 'save' him and, if you're being truly honest with yourself, his love will save you too.

In an ideal world, your boyfriend would learn from his experiences and realise that running away solves nothing and instead of making himself feel better with the attention of other woman understand why he is so empty inside. However, there is a bigger 'but'... The one that you end your letter on... he's got to want to do it (and not just for five minutes when he's feeling ashamed and you're in tears begging him to change). Otherwise you will be forever worrying: my man has a wandering eye and I've got to police him and stop him having another affair. It sounds like a recipe for more shouting and arguments rather than happy ever after.

Fortunately, there is an alternative (although I doubt it will appeal that much). Instead of trying to save your boyfriend from himself, so he can save you, why don't you put all that energy into trying to save yourself?

What do you want from life (beyond him)? How did you get yourself into such a bad place that running away from job, friends and partner seemed the only solution? Are you similar to your boyfriend that you close your eyes to stuff until it gets so bad that you're overwhelmed? At that point, you reach for any possible life raft (even if it's worse than where you are?). Are you true to yourself or do you do what other people want? As I've already hinted change is tough and takes time. You've got to understand the impact of your childhood on today, find ways of boosting your self-esteem yourself (rather than getting it from your boyfriend) and learn to be assertive.

When you have a better handle on who you are, what you need and can ask for it calmly and clearly, you can begin to decide if you want to stay in this relationship or not. You might decide that he's kind and fun (and you can turn a blind eye to his dalliances with other women) or that his 'love' comes at too great a cost. Whatever happens, you can't change him—only he can do that. But that's fine because you need to focus on changing yourself and learning to make yourself happy.

What is love? *Working with the reality of the situation rather than how we'd like it to be.*

45.

I have been with my husband for over 24 years. We have always had a healthy sex life and I thought were very much in love, although looking back, I knew something was wrong with our relationship and that he was becoming uninterested in me. In February, I found out he had been having an affair the previous autumn, from texts on his phone that he had forgotten to delete. The texts were long after the affair had finished, trying to placate the other woman as she had started posting abusive messages on Facebook.

When I found out I was devastated and, initially, my husband denied everything and said he had only texted and emailed this woman. I contacted her but she threatened to come to my work place and 'tell me all about my husband'. She knew I was a teacher and where my school was. The following day her ex-husband emailed me saying that he didn't want my husband to 'get away with anything' and wanted to meet me. I declined this offer but my husband then realised he had to admit to the affair. He said he had met her in a pub one night with a friend who was chatting to her friend. She asked his friend for his number and they agreed to meet up the following week. That night they met and went straight to a hotel. This happened on five occasions over three months, they never went anywhere together and only met at the end of the night and had sex in a local hotel. On the last occasion, she asked him when he would be leaving me and he said he would never and so he stopped seeing her. All of this seems so unbelievable to me, as I cannot imagine any woman being prepared to have sex in a hotel room with a stranger, in hope that they would leave their wife.

My husband has been truly shocked at the trauma that has occurred and how upset and ill this has made me. Initially, he said it was an affair that lasted for four months and now says it was only two months. I have tried to explain that this makes it hard for me to recover as I cannot make sense of everything and cannot believe he can't remember. We had been to couple therapy and he said he simply cannot explain why he did it, that he never stopped loving me, that I did nothing wrong and he doesn't know what he was thinking. He has not told any of his friends about the affair, although all my family and friends know as I wanted their support. I truly believe he will never do such a thing again, but I am grieving for a relationship that I think is so damaged.

Two weeks after I found out about the affair, I bought your book and read it from cover to cover and kept it by my side, often to support myself if having a bad day, as I really want my marriage to survive. I have stupidly looked this woman up online and I don't like her! She is genuinely the sort of person I would not have as a friend, and I think if that is the sort of person he likes, what does that say about me? I feel like I don't know my husband, all my friends are shocked and think it is out of character for him, but perhaps none of us know him at all.

I agree with what you say about how difficult divorce is, as my parents divorced when I was a toddler. Despite finding out about the affair over six months ago, I still think about it every day and cry regularly and worry that I am not going to be able to forgive or forget. I know you say it is not healthy to keep wanting to ask questions, yet I want to ask my husband the same questions over and over again. Does this mean I will be unable to recover and should accept that my trust and hope is crushed beyond repair? When do you accept that you cannot forgive and try to move on in life? I love my husband, but feel so betrayed and sad.

Andrew writes:

Six months is still early days in 'after affair' world. I would only be worried if you were still in the same place after two years (as it is important to get through the first of everything—your birthday, Christmas, discovery date etc.—and the second time round, you should be feeling much better).

In fact, if you cannot forgive I'd say fine, *accept* your feelings. You're feeling betrayed and sad (and for good reasons). However, I'd like you to *challenge* your thoughts—which are probably driving a lot of your feelings.

For example, you are worried that your husband decided to have cheap sex with a woman that you wouldn't like or respect. You ask what that says about you? I would say nothing very much! Why would a heterosexual woman expect to be able to predict what a drunk man in a pub fancies when it's offered on a plate?

Perhaps you think you should be able to read his mind? If that's the case, I would question whether that's healthy as it can lead us to making all sorts of conclusions... like 'he should also read my mind and know when I needed extra support (so I don't ask for what I need)'. It also sends people in the direction of thinking: we have to be totally alike, have the same tastes in music, hobbies etc., and be two peas in a pod. Unfortunately that can easily tip over into being controlling (telling each other you don't want to do that) or becoming too alike (and that can tip over into being brother and sister).

If you challenge your thoughts, like I just did, you'll probably realise that this woman says little about you (and ultimately not that much about him). You could find that not really knowing him is challenging (I've a lot to learn about relationships) or interesting (maybe he's more complex than I thought) or you could find it threatening (hence the pain and betrayal). See how your thoughts colour your emotions.

Next, look at why you want to know the answer to these questions. Do you think 'if only I can understand' then I can move on? I spend a lot of time with women trying to help them with this goal. Sadly, it is often impossible because most woman simply can't get their head around cheap sex in a hotel because it's something they would never do. Put simply, you're not him!

Ultimately, love needs *skills* and connection. And that's the great part of all this! If you improve your relationship skills (rather than just be alike or knowing everything about each other) you will improve your communication skills and therefore your marriage (and stop this from happening again). Be patient with yourself, get reading, brush up your skills and see how you're feeling in six months time. I hope it will be a whole lot better.

What is love? *Celebrating the differences as much as the similarities.*

46. I have been with my boyfriend for nearly seven years, we have lived together for four. I fell deeply, madly in love at the beginning of the relationship, and for me it continued throughout. We were in our early twenties when we met and my boyfriend was not as experienced in life or relationships, so, through no fault of his own, was not as mature. From about two years in, I knew I wished to settle down and have children eventually with this man. However, he was non-committal with his feelings, procrastinated and because he is quite a reticent guy, the building blocks of a life together—like shared hopes and dreams—seemed out of reach to me, which I found very difficult.

A year ago, my boyfriend proposed completely out of the blue in the most perfect way. I was so so happy, he had been so reluctant in the past that I was thrilled when the day came. Six months after the proposal, the same deliberation around the wedding plans ensued, I was tired of being the driving force, and we starting arguing a lot. Then the old text book happened and I was pursued by and had an affair with a very unsuitable party. All the things I had found hard in my 'proper' relationship flew to the surface: the anger and resentment I had not realised that I had held inside so long overwhelmed me. I initially did not admit the affair but I was so cruel to my partner, who I love, I was really breaking his heart but could not see it. I went abroad, genuinely to sort my head out, even though he pleaded for me not too. I was out of control, it was like I stepped out of my body and mind. I wanted the affair to stop but I was so confused I did not know which way was up, so I came clean to my fiancé. He went berserk and left me.

As soon as I told my fiancé, the spell of this other man was broken—he repulses me. This was two months ago. To my ex-fiancé, trust and loyalty (quite rightly) is number one. Initially all hope was lost—he would not see me or return calls, and threw insults, through understandable hurt, fear and sadness. However, things have started to defrost a little and his anger has calmed. We bonded over simple, practical tasks like clearing out our joint home. Even though this was a heartbreaking experience, we were very amicable, given what happened. We are now living separately in the same city (his choice, not mine). I want to save this relationship and be with him, my feelings for him are truly re-born. He cannot get past the thought that if I can do this when I had just got engaged, I am not the type of girl he wants to build a future with and I feel it is this point I have to convince him on.

I truly broke his heart—I think just as he warmed up to marriage, I blew it. I know I am not a bad person or a serial cheater but a very stupid girl who made a serious mistake. I can see now, clearer than ever, the things to work on in the relationship, I can articulate my feelings to him like never before. He has admitted 'he can see he made errors, but nothing justifies what I did'. He has filled his calendar with things and I initiate all contact. However, when we do see each other the chemistry crackles, we hold hands and he has admitted his anger is lessening and he feels love for me. I want to fight for this relationship, but don't know how.

Andrew writes:

It is possible to recover from infidelity and end up with a stronger relationship than ever before. This is because, as you have discovered, all the hidden poison in the relationship—which has been lurking at the bottom of the pond—floats up to the surface. At that point, you can begin to deal with it. So how do you move forward from here?

Firstly, I think you should acknowledge that only two months have passed. It will take your boyfriend quite a while to build up his trust again. Secondly, I think you need to look deeper into your heart, understand what happened and why you decided to cheat. Owning up and admitting your mistake is the first step. However, I think it is important to understand why you succumbed to temptation—at the very point that you had everything you wanted! It is almost as if you panicked and sabotaged your happiness. I think you owe it to yourself and your boyfriend to understand why—otherwise, his fear will always be that it could happen again.

So what happened? My guess is that you were frightened. This is because although we crave closeness, we're also terrified of getting hurt (and nobody can hurt us like a loved one). So we lead a complicated dance, trying to get close and then trying to get a bit of space. It is always something to do with our past experiences. Has someone let you down badly? Did your parents get divorced? What losses and upsets have there been in the past?

You might think marriage will calm these fears and make you more secure. However, you're going to stand in front of all your family and friends and pledge eternal love. The vows are also legally binding and have a huge financial implication. If it goes wrong, being a divorcee has a stigma that doesn't come with splitting up after living together. Marriage is serious. Marriage is forever. That's right! There's goes your freedom. You can never sleep with another person—ever again. So you better be sure! And who is ever 100 per cent sure about anything? No wonder you panicked and no wonder your fiancé took his time deciding to pop the question.

So how do you rebuild the bridges? Your instinct to hold back is a good one. He needs to find his own way back to you. All you can do is let down your drawbridge and explain what made you panic. Next time you feel frightened, tell him about it. If you can talk about something it is never so scary and this honesty about everything from the small stuff ('I'm angry because you left your dirty plates in the sink') up to the big stuff ('We need to do something about our sex life') will lay the foundations for a better relationship

What is love? *Something precious that can be shattered by a moment's thoughtlessness.*

47. I am 40, my wife is 43, and I'm in turmoil at the moment. We have been together for 14 years. The first three years were amazing—she really was my whole world—I had never known or met anyone like her.

We bought our first house together after about two years. When I proposed, she was apprehensive at first as she had been married before and has two sons. We were unable to have children together due to her medical history, but I knew and accepted this when we first met.

Finances and studying/career changes meant we were together for five years before we finally managed to get married. The problem is that after we moved in together I saw a side to her I discovered that I really didn't like very much—I realised that she was insecure and needy, and I didn't know how to deal with this. I had never seen this before in her and I felt like my bubble burst.

It was very wrong, but the year before we married I ended up having a relationship with a work colleague. We didn't sleep together, but we did kiss and meet a few times a week for about four months. I ended this months before the wedding and kept it a secret for years—I didn't tell a soul and put it down to a stupid mistake because I loved my wife.

However, we have had lots of major problems in the last two

years—financial, family bereavement etc., and I just felt so hopeless. Before I knew it I found myself AGAIN having a relationship with a work colleague. It started with a silly kiss on a work's evening out—it was just pure escapism—something just for me—and I KNOW how wrong it was…

Again, we didn't sleep together, we just kissed and met a few lunchtimes. It wasn't about sex as I had a fantastic sex life with my wife, but I did think at the time I was falling in love with her.

I never thought about leaving my wife or the consequences if she found out and I never planned or thought about having any kind of future with this person. I just didn't think of anything at all.

My wife discovered the affair and I almost had a nervous breakdown—I never thought I would be caught. I tried lying to her at first, but eventually told her the whole truth, which I should have done in the beginning. I confessed to the first affair at the same time. I regret it so much, it was with someone who was a guest at our wedding, so my wife is understandably devastated. She feels like her life has been a lie for years.

I feel so guilty and shameful for all of this—I don't know why I allowed it to happen.

My wife and I are currently separated; she is attending individual counselling for her own personal issues. I know I am depressed and have been for about three years—and now intend seeking help for this. Our hope is to work through all this and end up together again. We are attending couple counselling again in two weeks time because we know we don't communicate or deal with confrontation; we just 'paper over cracks'.

I was never unfaithful to escape my marriage—I never even thought about life without my wife and family. I know I love and care very deeply for my wife but I think I should feel 'in love' with her. I'm confused because I still find her hugely attractive and want to make love to her and spend time with her—and we both know we have a very strong foundation to build on—so am I just looking for something which isn't there?

Andrew writes:

Congratulations on a very thoughtful and heartfelt letter. It seems after years of running away from yourself, you're about to stop and meet yourself for the first time. At the moment, you don't like what you see, but don't despair. Peeking through the letter is someone who wants to grow and become the sort of man that your wife deserves.

So let's start at the beginning, arguments are the key to a good relationship. If you suppress your disagreements and unhappiness, it just gets all blocked up inside and nothing changes. No wonder you have been depressed for three years. Depression is caused by shutting all feelings off (not just negative ones but happy ones too) and the feeling of hopelessness that nothing will change (of course it won't if all your feelings—the alarm bells that something is not working—have been disabled).

Instead of releasing the feelings and getting better, many people with depression choose to 'manage' it instead. Normally by self-medicating (blocking off feelings) with work, alcohol or in your case a self-medicating affair.

The next part of the story is when everything turns a corner. Finally, you tell everything. By making a full confession, you can start again. If you had kept back information, so as not to 'hurt' your wife (or yourself), she would always have had a nagging doubt and you would have spent more time stepping round the truth than dealing with it. (I've had couples that have prolonged their recovery by two years because her instincts told her there was something more but he kept back two extra one night stands.)

So what's stopping you from being truly in love with your wife? I think you need to get to know yourself a little better (although you've made a great start). So what might you need to uncover? When we find something distasteful about our partner, more often than not, it's actually about ourselves. That's because, firstly, we suppress the bits of us that we don't like and, secondly, further distance ourselves by being hyper-vigilant and critical of anyone else who displays these forbidden traits. As you were uncomfortable about your wife being 'insecure and needy'—perhaps there's a dash of those qualities in you too? (Welcome to the human race. We all feel like that from time to time!)

How do you climb out of this? You've made a good start and counselling will help (although be prepared for things to get worse before they get better). I think better communication between you and your wife will help and if there's anything positive to say about an affair is that it prompts both more talking than most couples have done in years and looking deeper into your psyche than ever before. So grab this opportunity to learn and grow. There's a tough journey ahead but I have a sneaking suspicion that you can make it.

What is love? *Being part of something bigger than yourself.*

FINDING LOVE AGAIN

48. It is nice to write to you with hope.

My partner and I have started to see a therapist and discovered that we both needed some space. So we've decided to move apart in the coming months but stay in our relationship—simply take a step back and 'date' each other again.

We discovered we both moved very quickly into our relationship (no break between partners) and now just want to take some time out to rediscover each other and ourselves again.

As you mentioned in your books, we have set a time frame and have agreed a month when we can re-open the idea of us moving back together. The new blossoms you mention are coming out— we suddenly feel different to each other. We both see a light at the end of the tunnel again.

Our places are not going to be ready for another two to three months, so in the meantime I don't want to cause the new buds of love to die again. We struggle with loving attachment, are there any more tips that you have to build this stronger for us and keep us going good until we get the chance to move out. Also, I know my issue is that I tend to cling and suffocate. I am scared that by seeing such positive changes, I will once again fall into old shoes. But, I am being very careful with my reactions.

Once again, thank you for your help. I think for me, your books have helped me through the last few months and also to help accept the process we are going through in therapy. I now see the negative things said as positives because it is a chance for us to finally clean the closet.

Andrew writes:

I'm really glad that you and your partner have turned a corner and that you're feeling much more positive again. Congratulations on your new outlook.

So what do I suggest for helping along your new buds? Firstly, relax and enjoy the improvements. Don't beat yourself up for wanting to be close to your partner. We set so much store today by freedom, standing on our own two feet and being master of our own destiny that we lose sight of the importance of interdependence, selflessness and working towards something bigger than ourselves.

Ultimately, every relationship needs two things: closeness and distance. Without the first, there is no relationship. Without the second, we get swallowed up and lose our personal identity. In an ideal world, each partner is responsible for both halves. However, sometimes people get polarised into campaigning for just one end of the spectrum—for example, independence. Meanwhile, the other partner holds all the commitment—and is forever frightened of being left.

At the moment, it sounds like you are in a good place and able to talk freely about your relationship (and your personal needs too). You feel there is enough closeness and he feels there is enough distance (so he can be himself). If, after you move out, the balance shifts and you're feeling uncomfortable and worried that you're not doing enough together, don't swallow your needs (and brand yourself as 'needy' and 'clingy'). Instead, tell him about your fears and discuss what you could do differently that will also respect his needs for space too.

What is love? *Communicating your needs, rather than ignoring or hiding them away.*

49. These few lines are to say *thank you* to you. After your answer to my letter, I made my decision: to divorce and find a new fantastic adult man to stay with for the rest of my life! But I hadn't read the last chapter of *I Love You But I'm Not in Love With You*.

The result is what you can expect: my husband came back to me after 10 months of total silence and after he felt he had grown up! He said he missed me a small amount every day and, at the end, he missed me so much he could explode!

So I have my fantastic adult man I always loved and he has the only woman he will love (and he is really sure of that)!

For the last few months, we have started living together again; we talk a lot and try to share our emotions and feelings. We spent our holidays regaining our fellowship and trust. There are some moments in which I remember my year spent without him, but he is with me and everything (sorrow, solitude, sadness) disappears. Now he desires that I count on him and I feel I can definitely do it: what a wonderful sensation!

Thank you again for your advice!

Andrew writes:

This is the most wonderful news. Thank you for the progress report and for giving hope to everybody else. I'm often faced by couples where one party says 'I don't believe that feelings can change' or worse still, 'I don't believe that people can change'. To the first, I remind them that they once loved their partner and their feelings have changed. And if I didn't believe that people couldn't change, I would have changed careers 30 years ago! So I always try and change the focus and get people to ask the question: 'How can I change my feelings?' Time and time again, if you can improve communication, the situation will improve and the feelings return.

Here's the original letter:

My husband left me three weeks ago after 12 years together. We are both 42 years old. Four years ago, he saw his father dying in the hospital from cancer. From that moment he changed his work from a manager of a big company to a lawyer with his own firm and started new activities: he wrote some short novels and had some prizes for them, he launched a website for legal jobs research and he decided to invest some money in the production of T-shirts with his own drawings on.

I was with him, encouraging him with love and actions (draft correction of the novels, advertising his website in the universities of the cities I reach with my work, giving him enough time to follow up all these activities). We were trying for a baby, but stopped when I had a drastic reduction of my salary, his T-shirt adventure was going not so good because of the crisis and he said to me 'I love you but...'. He told me he met me too early and he would like to have more experiences with girls and write his book.

On New Year's day he said he had decided to leave me and that I couldn't do or say anything that would change his opinion because he felt like he was in prison with me. He started to search for a beautiful flat in the city centre, with a parking place, with a very low budget. When I told him that if he felt in jail he should find the first available flat and go away, he answered he had all the rights to live in a beautiful place. He left soon after Valentine's day.

Now he seems more relaxed, although he doesn't want to go to a marital therapist or to a therapist. We phone each other often, talking about our daily lives, and we meet sometimes. He doesn't know the reason he left me, that he is sure it's through no fault of mine because he tried to name my faults but he couldn't. He feels confused, like in the fog, but is beginning to feel better.

Here is my original reply:

So what do I think of your husband? Reading your letter, I alternated with admiration for his industry (the books, the T-shirts and new business) and thinking he was a selfish bastard! My guess is that's how you've been feeling too. So now I've vented my feelings, let's take a step back and look at what's going on here.

It sounds like your husband is having—and here, if I was talking to you, I'd drop my voice—a 'mid-life crisis'. I drop my voice because everybody going through one will deny it. Partly because it makes us the butt of jokes, partly because it doesn't even begin to encapsulate the scale of what he's going through and mainly because nobody will accept that they're middle aged—and that's the problem. (So please do not say Mid-Life-Crisis to him under any circumstances.)

So let me try and explain what's going on. Watching your father die is a huge reminder that we are not immortal and it triggers an existential crisis: who am I? How am I going to make sense of my life? How am I going to leave my mark on the world? His answer has been to become creative and leave books behind and the most obvious solution: to become a father. Sadly, the two of you have had another 'bereavement' and had to grieve your children who will never be born.

Unfortunately, many men are not equipped to deal with the enormity of an existential crisis. They don't have the words or insight or believe they have to solve all their problems themselves and refuse help. Under these circumstances, the high of a new romance can seem like an easy answer. Worse still, many men begin to see their wives as a hindrance to finding the answer, not a help. I guess you know the rest...

So what can you do? It depends on how you see him. He is either a man in crisis (who needs sympathy) or a selfish overgrown teenager. (Personally, I veer towards the former but I'm not having to deal with the fallout!) If you think the former, keep the lines of communication open, be polite and nice (however tempted otherwise) listen without trying to fix (or suggest that he comes home). If the latter, you need to start distancing yourself from him.

Finally, you ask for my predictions. If you can stay his friend, there is a good chance he will discover that although life might be tough—it's a whole lot easier with a helpmate to share the ups and downs. However, he could also meet someone who will make him feel brand new again.

So have a good long think what kind of man your husband is. Then think about yourself, do you have enough love to give and keep giving (without any guarantee of getting a return)? When you've answered those two questions, you'll know how to move forward. Good luck.

What is love? *Being in it for the long haul.*

50. My husband of eight years (we have been together 19 years), had an affair under my nose for a year and a half. The marital home was sold and for the last year he has rented a separate property and continued his relationship with his affair partner, although she never moved in.

Their relationship ended and a month later he sought reconciliation with me. We have been spending an increasing amount of time together, mainly as a family as it is difficult to find time with our 15-year-old daughter and his long working hours; but taking time to speak with each other and to start working on our relationship. He has been making the right noises and slowly we have begun to make plans and discuss when we will look at moving back in with each other. It is the first time in two and a half years I have been happy.

Yet, since this weekend I have noticed he seems to be stalling. He has learnt in the last year that, for the first time in his life, he likes his own company. He needs some time for himself, be that to just catch up on things at his place or take an early night. He says he knows what he wants but needs to sort it out in his head and make sure it's right for both of us. I don't know whether he is now only just feeling the fall out effects from his affair.

Obviously I am now feeling confused and slightly anxious. I so want our marriage to work. Is his behaviour normal? Do reconciliations usually suffer set backs and appreciate slow careful handling?

Andrew writes:

I think that your letter will give hope to lots of other people—showing it is possible to find a way back after an affair. However, I'm not surprised that your husband has doubts. In fact, for me, it's a positive sign that he is voicing his concerns—rather than ploughing on regardless, trying to please you and ending up squashing down his feelings.

So how to reconcile after separation? I would hope that you would share his candour and talk about your fears too. In this way, you're both adults going into this together rather than him taking all the responsibility for getting it right. Ultimately, it has to work for both of you (not just you agreeing to anything to get him back). That's why reconciliation does need time, careful handling and taking away the ticking clock. So tell him, it's natural to have doubts and listen without getting upset, ask questions and discuss whether there's a way round them. Nine times out of 10, problems seem more manageable when they can be talked about. (And that includes your concerns that he's changing his mind.)

My one concern is that you're mainly meeting as parents and I would like time for *your* relationship to put down fresh roots. You need to be lovers as well as mum and dad. Otherwise, when your daughter leaves home—which at 15 isn't that long into the future—your relationship could be tested again. As I often say, marriage is forever but children are just passing through.

What is love? *Most appreciated when a couple thought it was lost for ever but subsequently found a way back to each other again.*

CONCLUSION

50 DEFINITIONS OF LOVE

1. More than just a blinding attraction.

2. A joint project where each partner is equally responsible for keeping it healthy.

3. Finding your other half.

4. More than just the absence of problems between the two of you but feeling truly connected.

5. Learning from your mistakes and trying to put them right.

6. Valuing differences rather than getting angry about them.

7. A balance between the heart and the head.

8. A skill as well as a connection.

9. Taking responsibility for our own stuff rather than expecting our partner to sort it out for us.

10. Patience.

11. Something that doesn't hurt.

12. A slow burning fuse as well as immediate fireworks.

13. Forgiveness.

14. A mirror that shows what you need to change in your life.

15. Being brave enough to ask the tough questions.

16. Stepping into your partner's shoes and imagining every word he or she says is true.

17. Something that grows as your family grows.

18. Love is effort with both partners regularly and routinely attending to each other's needs—no matter how they feel at the time.

19. Something that evolves and changes.

20. Making sex a priority.

21. Listening to what your partner has to say—even if it is upsetting—without cross complaining, getting defensive or shutting down.

22. Facing the negatives without fleeing or trying to impose a quick fix.

23. Trusting our partner is strong enough to cope with the truth.

24. Allowing yourself to be vulnerable enough to become close both emotionally and physically.

25. Something we have to give ourself as well as our partner.

26. Taking time to explore a problem and really understand where both of you are coming from before trying to find a solution.

27. Something that is not just black and white.

28. Showing your partner the real you.

29. One of the many feelings that we have every day, all of which need to be witnessed and taken seriously but not necessarily acted on immediately.

30. Learning to appreciate how your partner communicates his or her love rather than demanding it one particular way.

31. Wonderful but not a magic solution to all your problems.

32. Something we hardly notice—like the air we breathe—until it disappears. At this point, love becomes so obsessive and so all consuming that it is painful.

33. A gift that's harder to give to ourselves than to other people.

34. Something that can't be put on hold but needs to grow, mature and move onto the next stage.

35. Something that can be made stronger by adversity.

36. An equal partnership.

37. Opening your eyes to what's really going on.

38. Giving up your need to always be right.

39. Being able to give even when you're getting nothing back.

40. More than just a feeling but something that is followed up by loving actions.

41. Something that is always changing, growing and adapting as we mature and progress through the different life stages.

42. Both partners supporting each other and helping each other grow.

43. Staring into the darkness for long enough to discover some chinks of light.

44. Working with the reality of the situation rather than how we'd like it to be.

45. Celebrating the differences as much as the similarities.

46. Something precious that can be shattered by a moment's thoughtlessness.

47. Being part of something bigger that yourself.

48. Communicating your needs, rather than ignoring or hiding them away.

49. Being in it for the long haul.

50. Most appreciated when a couple thought it was lost for ever but subsequently found a way back to each other again.

SO WHAT *IS* LOVE?

I've spent the last 30 years helping people in crisis. Do they love enough to commit to living together, to marriage and to children? Can you reignite the spark? Is there enough love left to stay together? What if you love someone who is not your partner? All these life changing dilemmas not only for the individuals and couples sitting on the sofa in my therapy room but for countless unseen people—their children, their lovers and their extended families—who, to quote my clients, will be 'devastated' and 'heartbroken' or 'angry' and 'let down'. All those hopes, dreams, all that pain and betrayal, with everything hanging on one small word: love. You'd think they'd have a pretty good idea what love is. Except when I ask the person struggling to find a way forward what they mean by love, they look at me blankly, shrug their shoulders or come up with something general like 'a warm feeling inside' or 'a sense of connection'. Alternatively, I get some beliefs about love: 'it shouldn't be so hard' and 'if you don't feel it, well that's sad but there's nothing you can do'. Sometimes my clients just sidestep the question altogether: 'you know love when you feel it'.

I have some sympathy with their lack of words. Popular culture feeds us myths about love but precious little about what to do when reality fails to live up to our expectations (beyond find someone else and have another ride on the merry-go-round). There is also confusion because love is used to describe our feelings about our partner, our children, our brothers and sisters, our parents. You can also love your country, your maker, your best friend, your favourite music and your favourite foods. No wonder I get so many blank stares from the people on my sofa.

Fortunately, greater minds than ours have struggled with the question: what is love? So let's look at the ideas of a selection of thinkers from the ancient world to today's scientists with the technology to scan our brains and analyse our hormone levels. I will also throw my own thoughts into the mix and end with an exercise to help you pull everything together. After all, you will need a definition of love that makes sense of your dilemma and provides a resolution that you can live with.

The Greek words for love

The ancient Greeks had four different words to cover the range of emotions that we've packed into one.

Eros: Physical love. This love is all about passion, desire and longing and is probably at the heart of what my clients today mean by 'in love'. For the Greeks, it was about pure emotion without the balance of logic. However, Plato expanded the definition to include an appreciation of the beauty within a person.

Agape: Spiritual love. Whether this love is returned or not, it endures even without any benefits to the giver and regardless of the circumstances. The Greeks used agape to describe unconditional love for the gods. In some earlier texts, it meant a general affection or a deeper sense of love for your spouse (than the mere attraction of Eros) and for your children.

Philia: Mental love. This form of love is a conscious choice and has give and take. It covers friendship and your relationship with your parents and includes loyalty (for example, to your country). Philia is about virtue, equality and fairness.

Storge: Affectionate love. The natural love of parents for their off-spring. It was rarely used in ancient texts but included acceptance and putting up with a difficult situation outside your control (for example, the affection some subjects might have for a dictator).

C.S. Lewis (1898–1963) novelist, poet and lay theologian is best known for his *Chronicles of Narnia*. However, he also explored the nature of love from a Christian and philosophical perspective in his influential 1960 book *Four Loves* (Geoffrey Bles) which he defined as Affection (Storge), Friendship (Philia), Romance (Eros) and Charity (Agape).

Lewis considered Storge to be the basis for 90 per cent of all lasting human happiness. He considered it natural because it was offered without coercion and because it was based on familiarity and therefore able to transcend superficial qualities (like appearance and money). However, he recognised that Storge's greatest strength could be its weakness too and it could easily be taken for granted.

With Eros, Lewis was keen to divide 'being in love' and 'loving someone' from our 'raw sexuality'. He differentiated just 'wanting a woman' (what he called 'Venus') and 'wanting one particular woman' (Eros). This fitted with his theories of man as a rational creature with Eros including reason as well as instinct.

For Lewis, Philia was defined as friendship and was something to be prized as it was a conscious choice (rather than natural like Storge) or needed like Eros (in order to reproduce). He believed that we no longer appreciate 'the art of friendship' (unlike classical and medieval societies).

Finally, Agape was about Christian love which Lewis considered the greatest love of the four.

What we can learn

The Greek definitions of love broadens the debate from just passion (Eros) and includes qualities that we also prize: friendship, fairness and loyalty (Philia). Good relationships also have a spiritual aspect (Agape) so they transcend a simple conditional contract: 'I'll scratch your back if you scratch mine' (and if you don't I'll withdraw my love). Finally, we need acceptance (part of Storge) and the ability to endure difficult patches where, for example, our partner's mother has dementia and is focused more on caring for her than for us.

However, if love is going to include all these aspects we'll need plenty of self-knowledge (so, for example, we can recognise if our partner being less available has triggered abandonment issues from our past) and better communication skills (so we can raise any difficult issues, listen to our partner's viewpoint and find a mutually satisfying solution, for example, to scarce time resources).

Modern science

Developments in Neuroscience have provided us with a greater understanding of the brain and new ways of looking at love. Dr Helen Fisher is an anthropologist and a professor at Rutgers University, New Jersey (USA) and believes that love can be divided into three entities (and three brain systems which can operate separately or together in any combination).

Lust: Our craving for sexual gratification is accompanied by obsessive thinking and possessiveness. Even if things go wrong or we're rebuffed, lust just increases our desire. During this state, the brain is driven by dopamine, a neurotransmitter central to the reward system. Indeed, when scientists gave MRI scans to 32 people who were madly in love and showed them a picture of their partner, it activated the part of the brain that responds to the rush of cocaine.

Romance: Fisher considers this aspect of love more powerful than our sex drive: 'It doesn't have any facial expressions, it's very difficult to control and it's one of the most powerful neural systems that has evolved.'

Attachment: This is the sense of calm and security that you can feel for a long-term partner. It's associated with the hormones vasopressin and oxytocin which are responsible for the feeling of peace and unity after having sex together. 'I think attachment evolved to tolerate someone at least long enough to rear a child together,' says Fisher.

Dorothy Tennov (1928–2007) was an American psychologist who introduced the term 'limerence', after taking hundreds of testimonies about falling in love, and believed it was a distinct involuntary psychological state that occurs in normal people no matter what their background, culture or gender. Limerence, like lust, involves obsessive thinking about the beloved but unlike lust it is impossible to have limerence for more than one person at a time. Limerence comes with the ability to take even the beloved's negative qualities (he's shy or she drinks too much) and turn them into assets (I can bring him out of his shell or I can save her from herself). Meanwhile, with lust, it is possible to not even particularly like someone (just want to possess their body). Under the spell of limerence, all other problems fade into the background because you're either with your beloved or thinking about him or her and imagining what he or she would make of something. In contrast, it's possible to lust after someone without mooning over them.

Neither lust or limerence last forever. While lust is more fleeting, limerence can range from six months (when the feelings are not returned) up to around 18 months at full power. It gradually diminishes over the next 18 months and by three years, the blindness to every other attractive person in the world and the ability to see only good in our beloved have significantly reduced.

In my book *I Love You But I'm Not In Love With You* (Bloomsbury, 2006), I used Fisher's ideas of attachment and romance to describe what follows limerence. I called this kind of love: loving attachment. While limerence is unconditional, it can thrive even if your beloved does not know about your feelings or even your name, loving attachment needs to be fed (by listening, sharing, romance, body contact, supporting each other etc.). I also drew on some of the ideas from the Greeks, in particular Storge, to explain how it's possible to love someone (and care about their welfare) but not be 'in love' and talked about 'affectionate regard'. This is unconditional love similar to the feelings of parents for children but your destinies are no longer bound together (like with loving attachment).

What we can learn

Although knowing which parts of the brain light up when we're in love is interesting, it doesn't really move us forward. My theories about limerence, loving attachment and affectionate regard can explain what has gone wrong and help if you're prepared to hear my central message: *it is possible to fall back in love.* However, it is still a shock after the mists of limerence lifts and you see your beloved as he or she really is: which is that they are as flawed as you are. Yet what if your partner accepts that a relationship, or loving attachment, cannot be taken for granted—so needs to be fed and tendered, like a plant, or it will eventually wither and die—but still thinks there should be a natural connection too? As one man put it to me: 'Haven't you got to have enough desire to want to water the plant?'

The founding father of marital therapy

Up to this point, I have discussed what happens in our body when we fall in love and how our interpretations of love will guide our behaviour and the choices we make. However, a biological, historical and cultural perspective will not explain why we fall for one person rather than another. If you ask lovers, they will describe physical qualities that drew them to their beloved (a sexy bum or piercing blue eyes), qualities they admire (generosity, kindness or bubbly personality) or shared values or interests (both like going to the theatre or a belief in the central importance of family). However, there are thousands upon thousands of attractive prospective partners who have, for example, blue eyes, an outgoing personality and who are family orientated. If you push couples a bit further, they will probably say: 'we just clicked'. This might be true. However, it doesn't take us much further forward and this understanding of love leaves us incredibly vulnerable. After all, you could just as easily click with someone new and turn off your love for your long-term partner.

Henry Dicks (1900–1977) was a British psychiatrist and one of the founding fathers of marital therapy. He is perhaps best known today for his evaluation of the psychological welfare of German prisoners during the Second World War and for being the physician in charge of Rudolph Hess. However, he spent the bulk of his career at the Tavistock Clinic in London teaching, researching and seeing clients and wrote the classic text *Marital Tensions* (Routledge and Kegan Paul) in 1967. He came up with the theory of 'couple fit' to describe why we chose one partner over another. In a nutshell, Dicks believed it is down to both conscious and unconscious choices.

I've described some of the conscious choices and you can probably list all the reasons why you fell in love with your beloved, but by their very nature you won't know the unconscious reasons. So what could they be? I think one of the best explanations comes from a contemporary writer, Haruki Murakami (1949–) the Japanese author best known in the West for his book 1Q84: 'Anyone who falls in love is searching for the missing pieces of themselves.' So what do you need to complete yourself? Dicks believed that we all have a psychological blueprint based on our early relationships with our primary care givers. It contains all our fears, anxieties, hopes, dreams and our coping mechanisms and protections from day-to-day adversity. What makes falling in love so powerful is that our beloved is going through a similar unconscious process and finding their missing, interlocking and complementary needs in us.

What we can learn

In most cases, we are looking for our opposite to complete what we lack. For example, Sheila, 50, was a sensible woman who put duty, responsibility and doing the right thing at the top of her list of priorities. She had been to university and had a degree in teaching. Meanwhile, her husband, Derek, 44, was a bit of rebel, who had left school at 16 and did not sit his A levels until he was a mature student in his early twenties (shortly after he met and fell in love with Sheila). So what did each get from the other to complete themselves?

Dicks would describe the couple fit as follows: duty bound Sheila got a sense of flexibility and fun from Derek while he would have got stability and predictability from her. It certainly worked for the first 20 years together but by the time their three children were all teenagers, cracks in the marriage had turned to chasms. Derek fell in love with another woman and for months oscillated between leaving and wanting to stay. Eventually, he decided to give up his mistress, work on the marriage and start counselling with me. They could list all the pressures (financial and time related), issues in their sex lives (which needed updating after so long together) and disagreements about some of the specifics of child rearing (although they agreed on the fundamentals). However, it was more helpful to understand the tensions within the couple fit (or what is commonly called the chemistry, connection etc.).

There is a contradiction in finding your missing pieces in someone else and falling in love. More often than not, we fear the very thing that we need the most. (In popular culture, this is sometimes expressed as 'the things that you fall in love with are the very things that will drive you up the wall in the future.') I'll use Sheila and Derek to explain fully. Sheila's parents had strong views about right and wrong. She had to be picked up at 10.30 from parties and they thought TV was a distraction from school work (and therefore didn't have one). She was also the eldest and expected to set a good example to her younger siblings. There were no arguments with her father or mother who laid down the law and Sheila conformed, worked hard and did what was expected of her and in return her parents offered her lots of support, practical advice and a family first environment. Although Sheila must have longed to stay longer at parties or be able to chat with friends in the playground about what was on TV the night before, she equally didn't want to lose her parents' love and approval. So in her words, 'I was a good girl who did what I was told and without complaint.'

Meanwhile, Derek was the middle child of three and felt 'squeezed' between his elder and younger sisters. His mother had several nervous breakdowns and was heavily medicated for much of his childhood. Meanwhile, his workaholic father divided his time between a family business and being a church elder. As Derek explained, in counselling, 'it felt like I was jumping up and down saying "I'm here" and "I exist".' He started drinking at 14 and progressed onto marijuana and various other illegal drugs, but still didn't get the attention he craved.

So while Sheila might have needed to rebel and stand up for herself (to become her own person), Derek needed stability and security (so he could work out who he was, rather than just 'not like my parents'). In this way, they were simultaneously a force to balance each other out *and* equally each other's worst nightmare (i.e.: for Sheila, Derek was a school drop out and for Derek, she was teacher's pet who sat at the front of the class, knew all the answers and made him feel inadequate).

This is where we get to the truly magic part of love and the important insight of Dicks: we unconsciously find just the right person to help us grow. However, there is a downside. They will also test us—because growth is difficult, painful and extremely scary. In the early days, limerence and lust smooths over all the rough edges and hopefully we find a good-enough balance between completing and freaking each other out. In other words, we have a safe space to process conflict: both internally and with each other. In the process, we heal the inevitable wounds from childhood and hopefully find a better way of managing conflict from the example that our parents set.

However, life and circumstances can throw up problems—some of which we are conscious of and other are buried deep in our unconscious. In the case of Sheila and Derek, they had three teenagers who took up a lot of time and emotional energy and triggered Derek's old fears of being 'invisible' and 'squeezed out'. As well as these conscious issues, there were unconscious ones too. Their children were all going through their own version of rebelling/conforming and working out who they were and probably triggered similar mid-life questions in their parents too.

As well as completing us, there is a second complementary side to falling in love and couple fit. Our partner provides a chance to solve some of the dilemmas set by our childhood from our relationship with each of our parents and from their relationship with each other. The most common form, I see played out over and over again, is the anxious partner (who pursues their fleeing partner because they fear that they will never get the love that their distant, absent or rejecting parent held back) and the distant partner (who flees because they fear being consumed by the demanding partner because their father or mother was so over-committed that he or she was in every corner of their life or caused so much pain that their only coping strategy was to roll up into a ball and hope the problem would go away).

An example of this dynamic is Christina, 42 and Michael, 51. Christina's father had his first breakdown before she was born but she could not remember an incident until she was 12: 'He became really excitable, almost bouncing off the walls and started talking gibberish, and disappeared for several months, I was never told where he went but I guess it was some sort of institution. At other times, he would just stare at the walls for hours on end.' It was only more recently that her father has been diagnosed as bi-polar. In contrast, her mother was 'engaging' and 'likeable' and 'strong'. Christina admitted: 'Until recently I couldn't paint my mother in a bad light.' Meanwhile, Michael had an equally disturbing childhood—just in a different way. Although his mother was also 'incredibly strong' she was often absent through bad health and came from a tough working-class background. 'Her father was a shipbuilder, they were not a tactile family,' he explained. Michael's father was an alcoholic and his son never knew what mood he would be in: 'The house was tense and pressurised as we never knew when there'd be a nasty row.' Not surprisingly, Michael was a painfully shy child and withdrew into himself.

So what was the couple fit between Christina and Michael? Christina identified strongly with her mother and would have been very aware of her parents' dynamic: mother pushed for closeness, love and attention and her father was generally unavailable. Michael did not identify with either of his parents but had learnt to protect himself, in an uncertain world, by fleeing either physically (by being absent from the house as much as possible) or mentally (by closing in on himself and shutting down). For Michael, falling in love with Christina provided some of the missing pieces. She was more emotionally articulate, she wanted to be close and held out the promise of love, attention and acceptance. For Christina, Michael provided an opportunity to get the attention of a man who was clever (like her father) but also complex (like her father) and a challenge (like her father). However, there is always a downside. We might crave connection but it brings up our fears of being hurt, rejected or abandoned. In the case of Christina and Michael, he saw marriage as a suffocating trap (and had a panic attack shortly before their wedding) and she complained that he was always pulling away. However, there were enough good times in their relationship for them to have a daughter together and to be married for 13 years before seeking my help to discover if they had a future together.

So how do you use this knowledge?

When I explain couple fit, lots of people wonder if they wouldn't be better off with someone new, someone with whom they'd have a better fit than their partner. In some cases, this might be true. However, in my experience, our unconscious makes really good choices. Often what we see as a huge insurmountable problem is just us trying to grow and face up to our inner-devils. If you can learn some skills (like being assertive) and gain some knowledge (like a deeper and more realistic understanding of love), most of these problems can be overcome. There is another bonus—as well as a better relationship with your partner—you will make peace with your past and feel more comfortable in your own skin.

If you're still unconvinced about whether it's possible to improve your couple fit and a fresh start seems really appealing, it is important to stop and look at whether it really will be a fresh start. At this point, I'm going to introduce George Santayana (1863–1952) who was a philosopher, essayist and novelist and won the Noble Prize for Literature: 'Progress, far from consisting in change, depends on retentiveness. When change is absolute, there remains no being to improve and no direction is set for possible improvement: and when experience is not retained, as among savages, infancy is perpetual. Those who cannot remember the past are condemned to repeat it.' Santayana's idea has often been paraphrased as 'those who cannot learn from history are doomed to repeat it'.

So we might imagine that we'll find someone who will understand, accept and heal us but we are drawn to people acting out a similar psychodrama over and over again. Sometimes, it can seem different because, for example, you are being pursued rather than pursuing but actually it's still the same dance (and ultimately just as frustrating) but you're taking a different role. More often than not, once the limerence has cooled, you will be facing very similar problems as those in your existing relationship (but with added complications caused by a nasty breakup with your spouse and probably being older and poorer).

Perhaps you'd love a second opportunity with your beloved but he or she has a closed mind. In this case, couple fit is still important. Although it might be tempting to plunge into a new relationship, in order to feel better, you will be drawn to other people dealing with similar baggage. It is much better to work on yourself, increase your self-knowledge and reach a better place because you will attract and be attracted to other people who are in a good place.

My definition

We've considered the evidence from 50 different people grappling with love and some of the greatest minds from the ancient world through to today. I've tried to use my knowledge gained from over 2000 clients and 30 years of study to throw light on the different aspects of love. At this point, I think I should stick my neck out and give my definition. Here is my answer to the question, what is love?

Connection + Skills + Attention = Lasting Love

In other words, you need some chemistry (both conscious and unconscious) but also the ability to ask for what you need, listen to your partner's needs and negotiate when there is a clash (assertiveness) and finally, whatever you give your attention to is what thrives (being mindful).

YOUR DEFINITION OF LOVE

Ultimately, my voice is just one more in the debate. It is up to you to come up with your personal definition of love—one that you can live by and makes sense for your experiences. Therefore, I want to turn the question back to you. What do you think love is? To help with this task, I have an exercise to focus your thoughts and examples from clients of what they discovered.

Before the crisis

Imagine that you have a time machine and could go back to before the crisis that made you buy this book. (If you started reading out of intellectual curiosity or because you're studying to become a counsellor or to hone your counselling skills, either go back to before you picked up the book or to an important watershed in your life.) Ask the old you these questions and write down the answers.

If pressed for an answer, how would you have defined love?

Where did you get those ideas from?

What did you take from your parents and other significant people from your childhood?

What messages were you given by popular culture about love?

What strong feelings do you associate with love and marriage?

Don't worry if the answers don't make immediate sense or are contradictory, just write everything down like you're taking dictation.

Right now

Although your crisis is probably not over yet, a lot has happened and it has made you start to look at your life in a different way. To help capture this point on your journey, please ask yourself the following questions. I'm interested in how you feel on an average day—rather than on a high from a piece of good news or a low from a setback.

What have you learnt about yourself?

What have you learnt about love from recent events?

What ideas and stories in the book stick in your memory?

What old ideas of love would you like to discard?

What, in your opinion, is love?

Once again, don't think too much, just write down the first thoughts that come into your head but please make you answers as detailed as possible.

Moving forward

I have three final questions:

What have you learnt from doing this exercise?

What would you like to do differently from now onwards?

What would help you to deliver this resolution?

If you're not certain what I mean by the last question, this could be the support of your friends, going into therapy, joining a mediation group, going running, a weekend away or reading more informative books.

Summing up

There are no right or wrong answers. You know what's best for you because you're the world's expert on you. To honour your definition, please write it in this book:

What is love?

Your answer:

Alternatively, you could post your definition on Pinterest, Facebook, Twitter #whatislove (or your preferred social media). You will find me on all three sites so please follow, like or link to me and share your definitions. In this way you will further the debate and help other people asking: What is love?

APPENDIX

Other readers' definitions of love

To demonstrate how the exercise at the end of this book can help on your journey, I sent it to someone who has read my books and regularly posts comments on my website (about his progress dealing with his wife's affair). My thanks to him for letting me share his answers.

Before the crisis

If pressed for an answer, how would you have defined love?

To me love was that feeling you get, like butterflies in the stomach, when you first fall for someone. Love was also just 'knowing' that you love someone but couldn't put a finger on 'it'. Love also equalled sex.

Where did you get those ideas from?

I believe my ideas of love came from the world around me (movies, Valentines Day, TV etc.) and most certainly my parents (who rarely expressed love for each other).

What did you take from your parents and other significant people from your childhood?

Unfortunately, a lot. I've come to realise that my ideas of love and my behaviour has been heavily influenced by my parents who were never very affectionate, didn't communicate well (with anyone), and suppressed all their feelings until they came out in one big burst.

What messages were you given by popular culture about love?

I believe popular culture showed me that love was about a hero and a damsel, gift giving, romance, and seduction to name a few. I saw this in TV and Movies, Advertisements, Music, even school when we had Valentines Day dances growing up. Disney has made billions off love and I see my daughter being influenced by it every single day!!!

What strong feelings do you associate with love and marriage?

I had always associated Limerence with love and marriage... I was naive enough to think that was how you were supposed to feel a majority of the time. I also associated the concept 'best friends' or the feeling of being 'connected' with marriage. Also, the feeling of knowing that whatever happened in my personal life, I always had the safety of marriage to fall back on to. Love was also about fun... simply having fun and laughing out loud. Marriage was about commitment and no matter what, that commitment would never be broken. Marriage and love were about forever, the feeling of certainty.

Right now

What have you learnt about yourself?

I have learned that I have low self-esteem and I can be a very weak person. I caved in on myself rather than vent my anger at my wife for breaking our most sacred vows in marriage. I still keep it in and let her 'get away with it' today because I'm afraid she will run away and I don't want to rock the boat.

I have learned that I am also strong in many respects. Despite advice, I fought off depression for five months without the use of prescription drugs. I swallowed my pain and desire for revenge and never became vindictive after my wife's affair, which literally brought me to my knees and that took determination.

I have learned that I was just 'going through the motions' in life and marriage. I needed a wake up call, just not this one.

I have learned that if I am betrayed again, I can survive and that I will stand up for myself.

I am a loving, caring and deeply emotional guy, which is ok.

I am learning that other people's problems are not mine to carry or solve. I can only control myself but I can influence others around me through my thoughts, feelings, and behaviours.

I have learned that life isn't defined by crosses but rather our responses to them.

What have you learnt about love from recent events?

Love is not like breathing, it doesn't happen unconsciously. Rather love is like your brain, you must work on it, improve it, and it must be conscious. As soon as you take love for granted you are doomed.

Love is a myth...

Love is fragile and unless you secure it against the harsh winds of life the walls will come tumbling down.

Love is painful but worth it.

Life without love is like an oyster without a pearl. You are empty inside but if you give love time and attention you can create something beautiful.

Love is a great excuse and it blinds us to our failures.

What old ideas of love would you like to discard?

I have discarded all my old ideas of love and I am determined to redefine it and the role it plays in my life:

Love is not a fairy tale, love requires dedication and consciousness.

You do not need to be loved to love in return.

Love is not sex.

Love does not necessarily last forever.

Love is not constant.

Love is not a word or a feeling (it is a conscious state of mind).

Love is not created in the vacuum of space and appears out of nothingness such as the Big Bang.

Love develops over time, under the right conditions, and with the right attention much like the world around us.

What, in your opinion, is love?

Love is about being true and honest with oneself.

Love is about being vulnerable; about being seen and heard no matter the consequences.

Love is a rubber crutch. If that is all you have to lean on then you will fall over.

Another reader's definition of love

To provide another perspective on love, I asked an international business woman, in her mid-fifties, a mother of five and a Muslim wife who has attended my workshops and had therapy with one of my team for her definition of love before starting on her journey and now. My thanks to her for letting me share her thoughts.

Love before and after

Defining love is not easy. It depends on many things. It depends on your mental and emotional status when you want to think or write about it, your level of maturity and your knowledge of human nature, psychology and relationships. Simple definition of love as I always thought of it is the feeling of joy and happiness when you are with someone. It is related to romance and loving to be with a person as long as possible. Expressing love is a big part of it (presents, candles, exchanging love words) and of course respect, listening and understanding ones' needs.

To me, love is an emotional feeling that we feel towards another person. It is a physical and psychological attraction and the desire to be with, close to, and intimate with another person. Sometimes it starts with preliminary attraction and develops into deeper love. It is the second stage that requires more than just the feeling but the ability to communicate with each other (not necessarily physical although it is the ultimate wish for both, but this is governed by the social and cultural context they are living in). Here a demonstration of each other's skills, understanding of life matters, their perception of relationships, their value system are put under the test. Marriage is another level of relationships. It could be the third level of a love relationship with more commitment or just a relationship with a different purpose. The purpose of marriage is different from one person to another and is also very much influenced by culture, religion and media.

In Islam and other religions too, marriage is mainly initiated to create a family. Preventing men and women from adultery, managing desires and putting it in a formal context as well as having children to extend the family and preserve human race. Maintaining a good relationship with one another is important but emotions have no mention here. They are left to the persons involved. They usually say love comes after marriage. In our religion, if this does not happen 'do your best', if you cannot, you can simply choose another partner. Men have more choices and it is much easier. The door is open for three more (or even more as long as you do not exceed four at any time). Although religion has stated many conditions to that (i.e. difficulty in the marriage, sterility etc.), it has never been explicit in the Holy book (The Quran) and is left for interpretation by religious figures and law makers based on the principals of our religion). Women are also allowed to choose another husband but of course after divorce. They are more restricted in terms of selection of a new partner and granting her a divorce. Decisions are made in court and by the court. Therefore, marriage relationships are bound by social and religious contexts in our and I guess in every society.

Some marriages are, or become with time, more of a function. It is more about roles and responsibilities. Some people accept that role and just live for the day. Each partner here has his own life, with few things to share. Emotions are not of much value here. I guess many marriages end up like this, but how fast and to what extent, it is different according to individuals.

To me marriage is much more than just a love relationship even if the two parties were living together before. It is the extent of blending and commitment that makes the difference. In marriage more commitment is required and expected. Here we talk about a 'family'. The complicity of commitment includes responsibilities towards one another, their home, their parents and friends, other people, their children and many other things which make the relationship more complicated. However, the level of blending is still different from one couple to another depending on how they both view marriage. For some, the blending level is high. They share many things including their family, social and financial responsibilities, leisure times, and face life problems and difficulties together. They both allow space but they also agree on the amount of space given and which both are happy and comfortable with. They resolve their differences with a high level of respect and understanding of each other's needs. They accept mistakes and apologies. They care about each other and each other's needs.

Emotions are very important in marriage, where each party loves to be in the company of, and is physically attracted to the other person. When all the other elements of success described above are there, love is sustained. I call this marriage as the 'ideal marriage' not because they don't face problems but because they have the ability to resolve them efficiently. A couple can reach this point when they both have the same level of commitment, skills, knowledge in relationship matters and is able to practice it. As they say 'It requires two hands to clap.' When both or one party declines to reach that, it becomes more difficult to continue.

Marriage problems occur when one party or both are not happy about what the other person is providing or not providing. Some people require more attention than what has been given, some require more freedom than they have. When the other party is not accepting or cannot provide, this becomes a major obstacle unless they reach a compromise that satisfies both.

I believe that cultural difference, media, personal experiences, religion and level of education and awareness very much influence the way we view and practice love, marriage and men-women relationships. My perception of love has changed a lot. It has become much clearer and precise. I can understand it more, and try my best to pass this knowledge to as many people as I know.

FURTHER READING

I Love You But I'm Not In Love With You

If you or your partner has fallen out of love, this book will explain why and set out a plan for rescuing your relationship. There is more information about limerence, loving attachment, the stages of love and love languages. It will also help you to...

♥ Argue productively and address the core of the issue

♥ Employ the trigger words for more effective communication

♥ Find a balance between being fulfilled as an individual and being one half of a couple

♥ Take your sex life to a deeper level of intimacy

♥ Create new bonds instead of searching for old ones

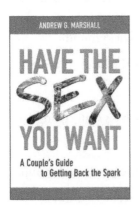

Have The Sex You Want

If your sex life is more about going through the motions, something you only get round to a couple of times a year or is just another item to tick off your 'to do' list, this book is for you. It will help you challenge the myths about sex that are stopping you from passionate love-making, break down the bad habits that have accumulated over your years together and rebuild your sex life into something sensual and more plentiful. I show how you can:

♥ Talk about sex with your partner without getting defensive.

♥ Deal with different levels of desire.

♥ Understand the three types of making love and how they can rekindle desire.

♥ Repair the damage from an affair by reconnecting again in the bedroom.

My Husband Doesn't Love Me And He's Texting Someone Else

If your husband has turned into a stranger, seems irritated all the time and nothing you say or do seems to make any difference, this book will help make sense of what's happening. It explains why men fall out of love and the three things every woman needs to know to protect her relationship. It is also full of practical techniques for coming back from the brink—like assertiveness—and advice on diagnosing whether your husband is depressed (plus what to do if he is). In the second half of the book, I tackle what to do if you suspect or know there's another woman in the background:

♥ The six types of other woman, from 'a spark' to 'the love of his life'.

♥ Tailored strategies for dealing with each type.

♥ Five worst and best reactions after uncovering what's really going on.

♥ How to keep calm even when provoked.

♥ How to combat the poison that she's slipping into your relationship.

♥ When to keep fighting and when to make a tactical withdrawal.

My Wife Doesn't Love Me Any More

If your life is in turmoil because you wife has just told you that she doesn't love you and your marriage is over, this book will bring a bit of sanity into your world. In my experience, more relationships end at this point not because women are determined to leave but because men panic and end up pushing their wife even further away. In this book, I explain how to keep calm and listen, really listen rather than arguing or trying to find a magic fix. I also cover: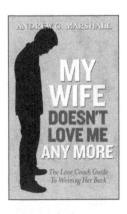

- ♥ How to figure out why she's fallen out of love.

- ♥ Five things you think will save your relationship but should absolutely avoid.

- ♥ What her words and actions really mean and how to use them to win her back.

- ♥ What to do to instantly improve the atmosphere at home.

- ♥ How to prevent past mistakes from undermining your attempts to build a better future.

- ♥ Five pick-me-up tips when you're down and need to keep focused.

- ♥ When it's time to admit it's over and what factors indicate you should still fight on.

How Can I Ever Trust You Again?

There are few things more traumatic than discovering your partner is having an affair. However, it is possible to come out of an affair with a stronger and better marriage. I explain the seven stages from discovery to recovery and the main reasons couples get stuck along the way. There's more information about Transactional Analysis (TA), making a Fulsome Apology and rebuilding trust. I also cover:

♥ The eight types of affairs and how understanding your partner's is key to rescuing your relationship.

♥ How to stop your imagination running wild and your brain going into meltdown.

♥ How the person who had the affair can help their partner recover.

♥ What derails your recovery process and how to get your marriage on track again.

I Love You But You Always Put Me Last

One of the key reasons why couples become estranged is that they put so much energy into raising their kids that they neglect their marriage. However, you don't need to choose between a happy marriage and happy children, you can have them both. I explain how to parent as a team and raise an emotionally healthy family. Packed with tips, advice and compelling examples, this book will equip you to turn your marriage round. I explain how to:

- ♥ Ask for the support you need.

- ♥ Overcome differences in parenting styles and find acceptable compromises.

- ♥ Share household responsibilities effectively.

- ♥ Define what your children truly need from you.

- ♥ Rekindle your passion for each other and keep it alive.

- ♥ Avoid the pitfalls of raising 'red-carpet kids' and give your children a strong foundation for the future.

Learn To Love Yourself Enough

If you're in the middle of a relationship crisis, it's easy to think everything would be better if only my partner would... However, that closes off one of the most powerful and effective ways forward: working on yourself. After all, if you are calmer and in a better place, you will communicate better and the dynamics of your whole relationship will change. In this book, I will help you step back, get to know yourself better and rebuild your shattered self-confidence. It covers how to:

- ♥ Examine your relationship with your parents: Discover the six types of child-parent relationships and how to accept the legacy of your past.

- ♥ Find Forgiveness: Debunk the two myths about forgiveness and discover what can be gained from negative experiences.

- ♥ Don't let other people put you down: Recognise the five phases of projection and how understanding our own projections leads to better and happy relationships.

♥ Re-program your inner voice: Identify the three kinds of negative thinking that work together to undermine self-confidence and whether they are based on fact or just opinion.

♥ Set realistic goals: Learn how perfectionism undermines self-esteem.

♥ Re-balance yourself: Understand that problems lurk in the extremes and why the middle way is the most successful way.

♥ Conquer Fears and Setbacks: Overcome the day-to-day problems that life and other people throw at you.

ABOUT THE AUTHOR

Andrew G. Marshall is a marital therapist with 30 years' experience. He trained with RELATE (The UK's leading couple counselling charity) but now leads a team in private practice in London and Sussex offering the Marshall Method. He is also the author of 14 other books on relationships and contributes to *Mail on Sunday, Sunday Telegraph, Times* and women's magazines around the world. To date, his work has been translated into over 15 different languages. To receive regular updates about Andrew's books, articles and events subscribe to his newsletter at www.andrewg-marshall.com

Other books by Andrew G. Marshall

I Love You But I'm Not In Love With You: Seven Steps To Saving Your Relationship

The Single Trap: The Two Step Guide To Escaping And Finding Lasting Love

How Can I Ever Trust You Again: Infidelity From Discovery To Recovery In Seven Steps

Are You Right For Me: Seven Steps To Getting Clarity And Commitment In Your Relationship

Build A Life-Long Love Affair: Seven Steps To Revitalising Your Relationship

Heal And Move On: Seven Steps To Recovering From A Break-Up

Help Your Partner Say Yes: Seven Steps To Achieving Better Cooperation And Communication

Lean To Love Yourself Enough: Seven Steps To Improving Your Self-Esteem And Your Relationships

Resolve Your Differences: Seven Steps To Dealing With Conflict In Your Relationship

Make Love Life A Prairie Vole: Six Steps To Passionate, Plentiful And Monogamous Sex

My Wife Doesn't Love Me Any More: The Love Coach Guide To Winning Her Back

I Love You But You Always Put Me Last: How To Childproof Your Marriage

My Husband Doesn't Love Me And He's Texting Someone Else: The Love Coach Guide To Winning Him Back

Have The Sex You Want: A Couple's Guide To Getting Back The Spark